# Developing Creative Talent in Art:
# A Guide for Parents and Teachers

D1521428

# Publications in Creativity Research
## Joan Franklin Smutney, Series Editor

*(formerly Creativity Research Monographs, edited by*
*Mark A. Runco and Robert S. Albert)*

*Achieving Extraordinary Ends: An Essay on Creativity*
by Sharon Bailin, 1994

*Beyond Terman: Longitudinal Studies in Contemporary Gifted Education*
edited by Rena Subotnik and Karen Arnold, 1994

*Counseling Gifted and Talented Children: A Guide for Teachers, Counselors, and Parents*
edited by Roberta M. Milgram, 1991

*Creative Thinking: Problem-Solving Skills and the Arts Orientation*
by John Wakefield, 1992

*Creativity and Affect*
edited by Melvin P. Shaw and Mark A. Runco, 1994

*Creativity in Performance*
by R. Keith Sawyer, 1997

*CyberQuest: Problem Solving and Innovation Support System, Conceptual Background and Experiences*
by John W. Dickey, 1993

*Divergent Thinking*
by Mark A. Runco, 1991

*E. Paul Torrance: The Creativity Man (An Authorized Biography)*
by Garnet W. Millar, 1995

*Eminent Creativity, Everyday Creativity, and Health*
edited by Mark A. Runco and Ruth Richards, 1997

*Everyday Frustration and Creativity in Government: A Personnel Challenge to Public Administrators*
by Thomas Heinzen, 1994

*Fostering the Growth of High Ability: European Perspectives*
edited by Arthur J. Cropley and Detlev Dehn, 1996

*Genius and Creativity: Selected Papers*
by Dean Keith Simonton, 1997

*Genius Revisited: High IQ Children Grown Up*
by Rena Subotnik, Lee Kassan, Ellen Summers, and Alan Wasser, 1993

*Developing Creative Talent in Art: A Guide for Parents and Teachers*
by Joe Khatena and Nelly Khatena, 1999

*More Ways Than One: Fostering Creativity*
by Arthur J. Cropley, 1992

*Nurturing and Developing Creativity: The Emergence of a Discipline*
    edited by Scott G. Isaksen, Mary C. Murdock, Roger L. Firestien, and Donald J. Treffinger, 1993
*The Person Behind the Mask: A Guide to Performing Arts Psychology*
    by Linda H. Hamilton, 1997
*Perspectives on Creativity: The Biographical Method*
    by John E. Gedo and Mary M. Gedo, 1992
*Problem Finding, Problem Solving, and Creativity*
    edited by Mark A. Runco, 1994
*Top of the Class: Guiding Children Along the Smart Path to Happiness*
    by Arline L. Bronzaft, 1996
*Understanding and Recognizing Creativity: The Emergence of a Discipline*
    edited by Scott G. Isaksen, Mary C. Murdock, Roger L. Firestien, and Donald J. Treffinger, 1993
*Why Fly? A Philosophy of Creativity*
    by E. Paul Torrance, 1995

**Forthcoming:**
*Creativity, Spirituality, and Transcendence: Paths to Integrity and Wisdom in the Mature Self*
    by Melvin E. Miller and Susanne Cook-Greuter

5- 24-02

# Developing Creative Talent in Art: A Guide for Parents and Teachers

by
Joe Khatena
and
Nelly Khatena

Ablex Publishing Corporation
Stamford, Connecticut

Copyright © 1999 by Ablex Publishing Corporation

All rights reserved. No part of this publication may be reproduced, stored in a retrieval system, or transmitted, in any form or by any means, electronic, mechanical, photocopying, microfilming, recording or otherwise, without permission of the publisher.

Printed in the United States of America

**Library of Congress Cataloguing-in-Publication Data**


Khatena, Joe.
   Developing creative talent in art : a guide for parents and teachers / by Joe Khatena and Nelly Khatena.
   p. cm.— (Publications in creativity research)
Includes bibliographical references and index.
ISBN 1-56750-407-8 (cloth) — ISBN 1-56750-408-6 (pbk.)
   1. Child artists. 2. Creative ability in children —Testing. 3. Gifted children— Identification. 4. Creation (Literary, artistic, etc.). I. Khatena, Nelly. II. Title. III. Series.
NX164.C47 K53 1999
155.4'1335—dc21                                      99–26305
                                                                CIP


Ablex Publishing Corporation
100 Prospect Street
P.O. Box 811
Stamford, Connecticut 06904-0811

*To our grandchildren, Paul, Joshua, and Jessica, and all the children of the world as they strive to develop and actualize their creative art talent*

# Contents

Acknowledgments **xi**

Preface **xiii**

**1.** The Creatively Gifted **1**

**2.** Measuring Creative Process **9**

**3.** Discovering Creative and Talented Individuals **27**

**4.** Art and Creative Imagination **41**

**5.** Related Dimensions of Creative Imagination **53**

**6.** Imagery as Language of Discovery **59**

**7.** Art Composition as Design **81**

**8.** Creative Thinking and Problem Solving Applied to Art **91**

**9.** Art Processed by Other Creative Imagination Techniques **103**

**10.** Instructional Application in Art **115**

**11.** Producing Art Using Creative Imagination **127**

**12.** Analogy-Metaphor Making Art **145**

**13.** The Magic of Color **159**

**14.** Evaluating Student Artwork **171**

References **181**

Author Index **187**

Subject Index **189**

About the Authors **193**

# Acknowledgments

We thank the various authors and publishers whose writings have been quoted in brief in this book. Furthermore, we are grateful to Mark A. Runco for reading the entire manuscript, making helpful suggestions to enhance the book and also for supporting its publication. We owe so much to so many for shaping our thoughts on the subject of the book and teaching us to understand how to develop creative art talent.

# Preface

We have written *Developing Creative Talent in Art* as a guide for parents, teachers, and others interested in developing creative art talent in young people.

Visual art has its own language system by which the artist communicates to others thoughts, ideas, and feelings about the world as seen through their eyes. First experienced as images and then codified using language, information about the world is processed by the creative imagination sometimes through the production of original artworks. Both the language of visual art and creative processing techniques are presented by example and instructional application so that students can compose art not only intuitively but also at will.

This book is based on the asssumptions that: 1) being able to recognize and know how to identify creative individuals with special talent in art, guidance can be given to maximize the achievement of their potential; 2) understanding creative imagination as process and skill will provide tools to talented individuals for their development in art; 3) mental images constitute the earliest informational source prior to their symbolization in one language form or another; 4) visual art has its own language, derived first from mental imagery, and just as someone learns and uses the language of words, the artist learns and uses the language of art in productive expression; 5) individuals can be taught to use creative imagination to process all kinds of information and its art language-imagery correlates to produce original works; and 6) feedback in terms of appraisal of student art is essential to foster and guide developing art talent.

We explore the nature of creativity and talent (Chapter 1); approaches to identify individuals possessing potential generally and in art specifically (Chapter 2 and Chapter 3); and the nature of creative imagination and its significance and relevance in art (Chapter 4 and Chapter 5). In Chapter 6 and Chapter 7, we discuss imagery as the language of discovery and the language of art and design as order and composition in art, respectively.

We explore creative thinking, problem solving, and other creative imagination techniques as processes and teachable skills applied to art (Chapter 8 and Chapter 9); instruction in how these techniques may be used to produce artworks with relevant practical exercises (Chapters 10, 11, and 12); the nature of color and its role in art production (Chapter 13); and, finally, approaches that can be used to evaluate student art (Chapter 14).

In closing, we hope that parents and teachers will find this book a useful guide in the education of young people to achieve their fullest potential as preparation for their emergence as true artists.

# 1

## The Creatively Gifted

### OVERVIEW

This chapter deals with creatively gifted individuals who are also talented. A creative and talented individual in jazz music and another in poetry are presented as examples. Many aspects of creativity have been studied, and as a result, measures to identify creative and talented individuals were constructed. In addition, training techniques have been developed to encourage more effective expression of creative potential.

### INTRODUCTION

One of the most interesting and fascinating subjects of human discovery is creativity—it can be attributed to the many inventions in all fields of endeavor that have made a significant difference to our lives. Hence, it is important that we make ourselves familiar with the nature of creativity so that we may not only be able to spot it among our fellows, but also provide opportunities for its development, enhancement, manifestation, and recognition.

### CREATIVITY IN JAZZ

My (Joe Khatena's) early awareness of creativity began in my teens when I first learned to play the guitar. To me, jazz was especially attractive, since with very little experience in music I could quickly be drawn to the melody and rhythm of songs. The simple sound and beat structures of jazz provided me with the framework for a great deal of musical flexibility. Once a tune and its chord accompaniment were learned, the way was paved for melodic and even rhythmic improvisation, or "ad lib," as jazz musicians would call it.

Clearly, to play a musical instrument one had to first acquire knowledge and skill in basic techniques. The student of the guitar who depended on learning by ear first, later acquired an understanding of how to play chords. Once some basic formations became familiar, the guitarist was expected to know how chords moved from one to the other in an orderly way. Such movement, consonant with the melody, was called "chord progression."

The next stage led to the playing of melody. With a grasp of chord progression, the melody could now be played with chord accompaniment, then began the fascinating part of playing variations of the melody in the context of chord accompaniment. At first, the easiest approach to gain competence in doing this was to listen to the way melodic variations are created by other jazz musicians in general and by guitarists in particular. Once one gets the hang of it, one could move from acquired skill to create one's own ad lib. To be able to play ad lib on a musical instrument quickly commands the respect of fellow jazz musicians, for not all those who attempt to do this are successful. Somehow, we interpret the ability to ad lib well as linking known music to the new or improvised. It involves a good feel or sense for imaginative music, and that makes this creative leap possible.

As it is in music, so it is in any form of art. What extends the boundaries to effect a transformation from a known art to the new is the creative impulse. It provides something that goes beyond the learned to precipitate new production. Preparation for such an event necessitates the acquisition of knowledge and skills in a specific domain. Once acquired, knowledge and skill serve as backdrop to the birth of the new; the agent that can accomplish this is creativity. Unlike the classical guitarist who plays music composed by another with very little room, if any, for creative rendition, the jazz guitarist engaging in ad lib composes in the act of performing. Composition for the jazz guitarist is creativity come to life.

## CREATIVITY IN POETRY

Creativity does not only affect the process of music, but also other language forms, words being one instance. Information reaches the individual through the senses at first as images to be codified as language symbols, then these are intellectually processed to produce information for communication. The processing may be managed by creative mental operations to transform the initial information into a new and meaningful communicable form.

Let us take the language form of poetry, for instance. It is not difficult to recognize that some of the most beautiful things we say derive their energy and effectiveness from creative imagination and the images they produce. Creative imagery often provides the artist or poet with the central idea for a picture or poem. For example, William Wordsworth's (1988) lament for someone whom he dearly cared is expressed in one of his poems composed in 1800. Images of nature provided the poet with information for analogical comparisons of beauty, transience, and permanence as central ideas for the following extract:

> A violet by a mossy stone
> Half hidden from the eye!
> - Fair as a star when only one
> Is shining in the sky. (p. 114)

Interpreted, the image of a violet against a mossy stone as background is naturally beautiful in color, texture, and vitality. It represents a girl (implied), as alive and within reach, although she may be passed by unnoticed ("half hidden from the eye"). Just like the violet, she is beautiful, royal, delicate, and transient. The comparison of the girl as a star shining singly in the sky not only reiterates the qualities described, but also presents them as gem-like. In this way, her permanence is tied to both immediate and remote aspects of nature. The imagery of the poem is congruent with the central idea of someone beautiful, once alive but now dead, transient yet permanent, transforming factual information into poetry (Khatena, 1978b).

Another instance of the workings of the creative imagination is provided by one of my (Joe Khatena's) own poetic compositions.

> Thoughts at Dusk
> *The stretched-out day draws to a close*
> *And golden glow behind tree-bordered lake*
> *Sinks rapidly into orange-grey hue.*
> *A single silent bird in querulous wire-perch*
> *Soon becomes indistinct against pecan-leaf posies*
> *That ornament lacy trees in darkness rush.*
> *Pollen patterned waters of stagnant lake*
> *No more visible had just before*
> *Been whipped to life by quickening breeze,*
> *And vibrant joy-peals of children at water's edge*
> *Ceased as the myriad insect night-chant*
> *Wooed light hours into natural rhythmic sleep.* (1981a, p. 47)

The central idea of the poem is nature's observance of the natural rhythm of day and night, wake and sleep, and its effects on natural surroundings. Poetic imagination transforms fact into lyrical beauty. The day "stretched-out" as if in repose, the changing hue of sunset from "gold" to "orange-grey," life in "patterned waters," "a single silent bird," and "joy peals of children" all diminish in intensity to become indistinct in "darkness rush" as nature prepares for insect song. Images like "lacy trees" and "pecan-leaf posies" enhance the lyrical quality of the lines, while the induced quiet mood is stirred to life by such dynamic images as "darkness rush," "whipped to life," "quickening breeze," and "vibrant joy-peals." The whole process of rhythmic change, indicative of natural continuance, is activated by an image of courtship such that "light hours" are "wooed" into "natural rhythmic sleep."

## THE MANY WAYS TO STUDY CREATIVITY

Creativity is a living and evolving subject. It has continued to be of great interest to psychologists and educators who have either addressed it directly in their own works (for example, Torrance, 1962), or indirectly as a contextual backdrop to comprehensive discussions on the gifted (Khatena, 1992). Interest on various aspects of creativity continue to find expression, for instance, in discussions on its nature and definition. Theoretical models have emerged that attempt to expand the conceptual frontiers of creativity. Facilitating and hindering environmental conditions have also commanded our attention. Furthermore, motivational aspects of creativity have also interested us. Other areas of study have included the identification of psychometric properties and how they have led to the development of creativity measures. The importance of creativity in various settings like education, business, industry, and management have led to the development of many training approaches and programs (see, for example, De Bono, 1970; Khatena, 1984, 1992; Parnes, 1988). That creativity is not entirely an individual phenomenon but one related to group-shaping influences led to its examination in sociocultural and developmental perspectives (see, for example, Arieti, 1976; Gowan, 1971).

Creativity has been of interest to many in the years prior to the 1950s, having sprung from Sir Francis Galton's study of hereditary genius. Early investigations focused on philosophical speculations and anecdotal reports of creative mental functioning. Take, for example, the German physiologist and physicist Hermann Helmholtz's analysis of his thought processes, later formulated by Wallas (1926) as the familiar four-stage paradigm of creative problem solving. This paradigm consisted of preparation, incubation, illumination, and verification. Grippen's (1933) study of the creative artistic imagination of four children between the ages of 3 and 7, Rossman's (1931) study of inventors, and Lehman's (1953) study of age problems and productivity are other instances of creativity applied to problem solving.

## PSYCHOMETRIC CREATIVITY

Adolescents and adults had to wait for theoretical constructs to shape instruments to measure their creative thinking abilities, because psychometric creativity had already put these tools in investigators' hands to measure these abilities in children. These constructs and relevant instrumentation were advanced by J. P. Guilford (1967) and

E. Paul Torrance (1962). Although the spirit of the times was an energizing factor for the study of creativity, the full impact of future directions of thought on the subject was precipitated by Guilford's 1950 American Psychological Association Presidential Address, entitled "Creativity." Guilford focused our attention on creativity and its social importance and educational implications—issues we had neglected hitherto. Guilford's newly discovered factorial model, "The Structure of Intellect," lit the fuse for the explosion of knowledge on creativity that to this day continues to break new ground in our understanding and harnessing of this potential.

With the advent of Guilford's model of intellect came the invention of a number of key instruments to measure divergent thinking or creativity. The main instruments constructed by both Guilford (1967) and Torrance (1962) and Khatena and Torrance (1973/1998a, 1976/1998b) depended on process for their constructs. In particular, these instruments consist of the Creativity Tests for Children (1973), adapted from adult measures described by Guilford, and the Torrance Tests of Creative Thinking (1966/1981).

Mel Rhodes's (1961) analysis of creativity categorizes identification approaches by person, process, product, and press to reduce the confusion level caused by numerous definitions of creativity. The development of several measures dependent on the construct of person was one result. Chief among such measures are the Khatena–Torrance Creative Perception Inventory (1976/1998b), and the Khatena–Morse Multitalent Perception Inventory (1994). The latter instrument, while producing an index of versatility, identifies leadership and several areas of creative talent, including art and music.

The other two identification approaches suggested by Rhodes (1961), product and press, have no instruments. The exception to this is the incorporation of elements of both in the person measures developed by Khatena and Torrance (1976/1998b) and Khatena and Morse (1994), as well as a procedure developed by Theresa Amabile (1983), which is based on consensual validation to measure creative products. However, while instruments on the measurement of creative potential based on the constructs of process and person will be dealt with here, Amabile's procedure for evaluating products will be dealt with in a later chapter, which focuses on the appraisal of artworks.

## CREATIVITY TRAINING

Once we begin to have a better understanding of the nature of creativity and approaches to identify creative individuals, we are led to consider how we may set about providing training materials to nurture the optimal expression of creativity. In an important article on the subject, Torrance (1972) summarized 142 studies, using the Torrance Tests of Creative Thinking as a measuring instrument, several different approaches attempting to teach children to be more creative were described. These included:

- programs emphasizing the Osborn–Parnes Problem Solving procedures;
- programs involving packages of materials such as the Purdue Creativity Program;
- the creative arts as vehicles for teaching and practicing creative thinking;
- media and reading programs designed to teach and allow practice in creative thinking;
- curricular and administrative arrangements designed to create favorable conditions for learning and practicing creative thinking;
- teacher–classroom variables, indirect and direct control, classroom climate, and the like;
- motivation, reward, competition, and the like; and
- testing conditions designed to facilitate a higher level of creative functioning or more valid and reliable test performance.

In another paper, Torrance (1987) presents an update of these observations that include teaching children and adults to think creatively. Added to the above approaches are those that involve the use of affective education programs, altered awareness states, meditation, and fantasy, as well as the use of complex programs involving several strategies. According to Torrance (1987), since 1983, trends in creativity training have included: a) increased attention to specific creative problem-solving skills; b) emphasis on cognitive theory and practice, guided fantasy and guided imagery, and thematic fantasy play and the use of games; c) training in creative writing to improve creative thinking; d) the influences of quality circles movement that bring into play intuitive abilities and future orientation to problem solving and planning; and e) the use of multiple realistic criteria to evaluate creative expression.

Among the most recent works on creativity termed as lateral thinking are *Six Thinking Hats* (1990) and *Six Action Shoes* (1992), both by Edward De Bono. Hats and shoes are useful symbols to activate thought and direct action. Idiomatically, the hat symbol is appropriate since we are quite familiar with the expression "put on your thinking hats (or caps)." Shoes imply action and direct attention to walking towards some destination. The colors chosen for the symbols label the kind of thinking or action to be done. Relative to shoes, De Bono presents six action modes, namely, Navy Formal Shoes, Grey Sneakers, Brown Brogues, Orange Gumboots, Pink Slippers, and Purple Riding Boots.

The six hat method is aimed at changing how thinking takes place, such that people are freed from back-and-forth arguments at meetings, for instance, for constructive discussion. Six colored imaginary hats are used, so that at any one time, a thinker may put on or take off a hat. The activity involves a participant in a kind of mental role playing. However, when a need arises for full and effective exploration of a subject, a sequence of hats may be put together, each used in turn.

As thinking must be put into action, the six action shoes method is brought into play. Shoes are for action. Just as different kinds of thinking are required, so different kinds of actions are needed to implement ideas and solutions to problems generated.

Consistent with Torrance's (1987) observation of current trends in training people to think creatively by using creative imagination and imagery, is some of my (Joe Khatena's) work, which has focused on several dimensions of creative imagination and its stimulation by a number of creative thinking strategies (1978, 1984, 1992). These have included the use of such approaches as divergent thinking processing images, synthesis-destructuring-restructuring, analogy, incubation, and sociodrama, as well as their educational implications. These will be handled in later chapters of this book.

What all this means is that we have learned that creativity does not need to be left to chance occurrence, but rather that many different tools have been shaped to encourage people to think deliberately in creative ways. By making such tools available, we are saying that we are taking control of an individual's natural predisposition to be creative and enhancing it to the fullest potential of expression.

## CONCLUSION

Creativity fascinates us, since it is the key to discovery and invention. In this chapter, we have described that creatively gifted individuals are also talented. Instances given illustrate such precocity in music and poetry. In addition, we have indicated that there are many facets to creativity and ways to study it. We can recognize creativity by measuring it and we can teach individuals to use their creativity more effectively. The next chapter presents several measures that can be used to identify creativity.

# 2

---

# Measuring Creative Process

## OVERVIEW

This chapter begins by describing four dimensions of creativity: process, person, product, and press. Among measures developed in the dimension of process are those by J. P. Guilford, E. Paul Torrance, and Joe Khatena. We describe measures developed by Guilford and Torrance, which relate to the nonverbal and verbal, and those by Khatena, which relate to the verbal.

## INTRODUCTION

Many people have shown an interest in creativity. Their attempts to understand creativity led to the production of many definitions. This gave the impression that there was disagreement about the nature of the construct, though if one takes a careful look at the definitions, one will realize that they relate to different facets of creativity. To give some coherence to the understanding of the subject, Mel Rhodes (1961) suggested that thought on creativity can be described as belonging to one of four dimensions: person, process, product, and press (abbreviated as the 4-Ps). This is to say that a person may show creativity in one of four different ways.

## CREATIVITY AS PROCESS

Creativity as process applies to "motivation, perception, learning, thinking, and communicating" (Rhodes, 1961, p. 219). For our purpose, we shall limit our discussion of process to *thinking*. One person may define creativity as thinking by analogy; another may define it as using initiative to stop thinking in tried or accustomed ways so as to allow thinking in new ways. Thinking of this kind can be expected to produce fresh relationships among things, either   consciously or unconsciously, leading to choosing or discriminating from many possibilities one that is most appropriate. Such thinking is aimed at synthesizing elements that hitherto have not been bound together in original ways. Of course, it is important to operationally define it before you begin measuring it. What follows are a few operational definitions of creativity that have led to the development of various measures.

Guilford (1967) defines creativity in terms of divergent thinking, which includes transformation, redefinition, and sensitivity to problems. Divergent thinking constitutes one of five inherited mental operations of Guilford's factorial model, "The Structure of Intellect."

Torrance (1962) defines creativity as the process of sensing gaps or missing elements and forming hypotheses concerning them, testing these hypotheses, communicating the results, and possibly modifying and retesting the hypotheses.

According to Wallach and Kogan (1965), creativity is the ability to generate or produce within some criterion of relevance many cognitive and unique associates.

Khatena (Khatena & Torrance, 1992) has defined creativity as the power of the imagination to break away from perceptual set to structure ideas, thoughts, and feelings into novel and meaningful associative bonds.

Rhodes (1961) has operationalized creativity as a person's traits, products generated, thinking process involved, and functioning under conditions of press.

Guilford, Torrance, and Khatena stand out as leaders in the measurement of creative thinking abilities. Their tests of creative thinking in general give major roles to four specific thinking abilities, namely, fluency, flexibility, originality, and elaboration.

*Fluency* is the ability to produce many ideas for a given task. Suppose a person is given the task of thinking of the many unusual uses of a brick. He may write "Throw it at someone, use it as a paper weight, use it to hold down a pile of clothes, coat it with chocolate and give it to someone as a birthday cake for a joke, and warm it on a fire to iron a shirt." The score in points is determined by the number of responses given. Here, the fluency score is five.

*Flexibility* is the ability to produce ideas that show a person's movement from one category of thinking to another, or shows shifts in thinking. Ideas that do the same job do not show shifts in thinking. For example, two of the unusual uses of bricks, "Use it as a paper weight" and "Use it to hold down a pile of clothes," are the same. That is, no shift in thinking has occurred. The remaining three ideas, "Throw it at someone," "Coat it with chocolate and give it to someone as a birthday cake for a joke," and "Warm it on a fire to iron a shirt," do different tasks, which show shifts in thinking. If for each shift of thinking one point is awarded, then for the five ideas produced, the flexibility score is four points.

*Originality* is the ability to produce ideas that are unusual, remote, and clever. For instance, when asked to use their creative imagination to process onomatopoeic words (shown in parentheses), highly creative people produced responses like "an ant walking on the icing of a cake" (murmur), "slushing watermelon through my teeth" (fizzy), "violin on a dog's nerves" (ouch), "barber cutting a man's hair quickly" (jingle), and "a frightened lizard" (zoom). One widely used scoring procedure for originality would award a maximum of four points on a scale of 0 to 4 for these responses. The scale is based on the principle of statistical infrequency and relevance, such that four points are given for very original ideas, to 0 points for common ideas (that is, generated by 5 percent or more of the normal population). The total number of points earned constitutes the originality score.

*Elaboration* is the ability to add details to a basic idea. Let's say a person is given a number of squares, told to think of new ideas, and instructed to draw pictures using the shape of a square. One idea for the drawing of a picture using a square could be a "door" (Figure 2.1).

If a person decides to add such details like screws and hinges, a decorative panel, extensions to the length of the door, and a name plate, he or she is elaborating on the basic idea of a "door" (Figure 2.2).

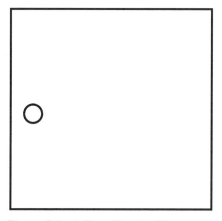

**Figure 2.1**  A Door. Reprinted by permission from Khatena, 1978a, p. 25.

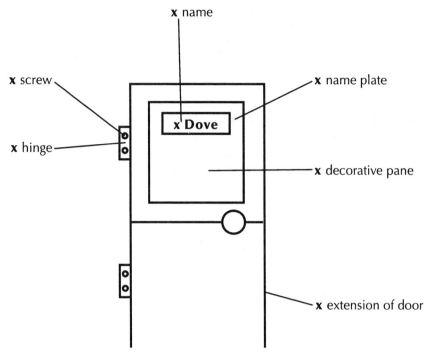

x name

x screw

x name plate

x Dove

x hinge

x decorative pane

x extension of door

**Figure 2.2**   Elaboration of a Door. Reprinted by permission from Khatena, 1978a, p. 26.

If one point is awarded for every detail added to the basic idea of a "door," the drawing should fetch an elaboration score of at least seven points (that is, each *x* on the picture indicates one point). It should be noted that the doorknob is not scored for elaboration because it is the first detail added to the square to give the door its identity.

Common to both Guilford's (1967) and Torrance's (1962) concepts of creativity and their measurement are fluency, flexibility, originality, and elaboration. Guilford measures these four abilities in a way that requires a person to do many test tasks, each setting out to give information about 1 of 24 divergent thinking abilities. Torrance measures similar abilities in a way that requires a person to perform several complex tasks, each designed to bring about a display of all these abilities simultaneously. While Guilford's measures apply to specific divergent thinking abilities, Torrance's measures identify creative abilities of fluency, flexibility, originality, and elaboration.

Relative to the test climate of Creativity Tests for Children (1973), Guilford indicates that the child needs to feel he is among friends when he is doing the test tasks. Furthermore, the child should be told that doing the tasks is like playing a game, since nothing is graded and therefore there is no such thing as "failing." Hence, enjoyment in doing these activities is the key consideration.

For the Torrance Tests of Creative Thinking (1981), Torrance recommends the creation of a game-like thinking or problem-solving atmosphere. The test-taker should not feel threatened, but encouraged to enjoy the activities. Furthermore, the psychological climate both before and during the test should be as comfortable and stimulating as possible. The cover of the booklet used in the test, with its apparently unrelated combinations of elements, is supposed to evoke curiosity, imagination, and interest. It is designed to facilitate or serve as a "warm-up" device, a feature Torrance considers essential to the testing procedure.

Both Khatena and Torrance recommend taking the Thinking Creatively with Sounds and Words test (1998a) in an atmosphere where good rapport has been established before the administration of the tests. A nontest atmosphere is to be created, whereby the test-taker is made to feel that using the imagination should be fun.

## CREATIVITY TEST FOR CHILDREN

This measure of creativity relates to the divergent thinking component of "The Structure of Intellect" model (Guilford, 1973). It is meant mainly for children in grades 4 to 6, although Guilford says the test may be used with older children and even adults. In general, the items are revised forms of the adult version of the divergent thinking dimension and are to be found in *The Nature of Human Intelligence* (Guilford, 1967). The instructions are rewritten in a way that children can understand. Although there are 24 divergent thinking abilities, only 10 of these are used for the children's test (Figure 2.3) and 18 for the adult version, which Guilford describes in his book.

Guilford's (1973) measure of creativity for children consists of 10 tasks, five verbal and five nonverbal, with each measure relating to one of the 10 divergent thinking abilities indicated in Figure 2.3.

The nonverbal tasks are called:

Making Something Out of It (Divergent Figural Units, or DFU)
Different Letter Groups (Divergent Figural Classes, or DFC)
Making Objects (Divergent Figural Systems, or DFS)
Hidden Letters (Divergent Figural Transformations, or DFT)
Adding Decorations (Divergent Figural Implications, or DFI)

The verbal tasks are called:

Names for Stories (Divergent Semantic Units, or DMU)
What to Do With It? (Divergent Semantic Classes, or DMC)
Similar Meanings (Divergent Semantic Relations, or DMR)
Writing Sentences (Divergent Semantic Systems, or DMS)
Kinds of People (Divergent Semantic Implications, or DMI)

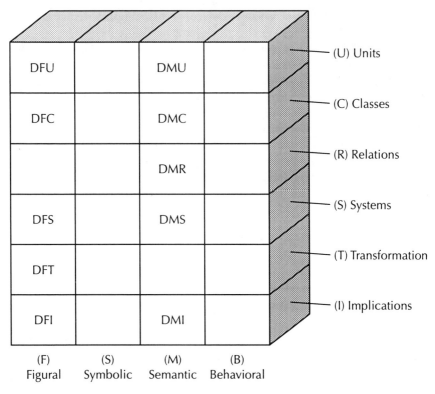

**Figure 2.3** Divergent Production Abilities. Reprinted by permission from Khatena, 1978a, p. 29.

**Nonverbal Tasks**

*Make Something Out of It*

This task provides the child with different figures or shapes. The child is asked to list the different things that can be made by adding something to each of them. The ability involves the ease with which ideas are produced. The ideas given must relate to the assigned shape, with no credit allowed for repetitions. See Figure 2.4 for an example.

The child listed leaf, buttonhole, spearhead, and mouth of a jar as things that relate to the shape in Figure 2.4.

**Figure 2.4**   Producing Ideas with a Shape. Reprinted by permission from Khatena, 1978a, p. 32.

### Different Letter Groups

The child is given the task of grouping and regrouping three capital letters from an assigned group of six letters that are alike in some way. For example:

C   I   F   L   G   Z

The child gave the following responses: ILZ (all have a base line), IFL (all have up-and-down lines), FLZ (all have a line going across), and CIZ (all are not alike).

The child is required to use the ability to make classes when given certain units of information, an ability that is very useful when it comes to recalling information from memory storage, where the search involves screening classes rather than units of information. One point is given for every new class of three letters made.

### Making Objects

The child is given the task of putting together simple figures or lines to make different objects. It is an ability that is used by artists, designers, architects, and engineers when creating products. Points are given for combining more than one figure or line to make different objects, with minor changes in size and position in the given shapes allowed. Take, for instance, a rectangle, a semi-circle, and a triangle (Figure 2.5), resulting in the pictures of a man, a car, and a face in a window (Figure 2.6).

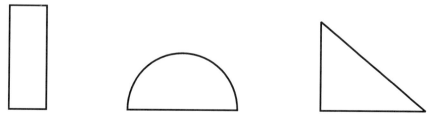

**Figure 2.5**   Three Simple Geometric Shapes. Reprinted by permission from Khatena, 1978a, p. 33.

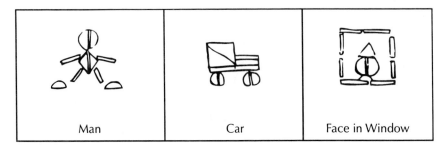

|        |        |                |
|--------|--------|----------------|
| Man    | Car    | Face in Window |

**Figure 2.6**  Composing Pictures with Shapes. Reprinted by permission from Khatena, 1978a, p. 34.

### Hidden Letters

A page of repeated and somewhat complex figures is given to the child, who has to find letters of the alphabet hidden in each of them. This ability requires the child to tear down the lines that make up the figure, then combine them into a letter of the alphabet, using the ability to transform information that is commonly known into something original. Many inventions have resulted from the use of this kind of ability. Each nonrepeated capital letter—in this case, N, X, and F—receives a point (Figure 2.7).

### Adding Decorations

The child is given simple drawings of familiar objects, such as clothing or furniture, and is told to add details to the drawing. This ability relates to seeing implications, the kind of work that an artist or inventor does in adding refinements to a

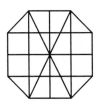

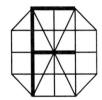

**Figure 2.7**  Finding Hidden Letters in Complex Figures. Reprinted by permission from Khatena, 1978a, p. 34.

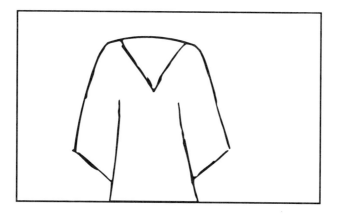

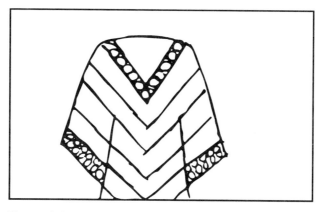

**Figure 2.8** Adding Details to Decorate a Simple Drawing. Reprinted by permission from Khatena, 1978a, p. 35.

previouly created product. A point is given to each decorative idea that has not been repeated. See the example in Figure 2.8.

## Verbal Tasks

### *Names for Stories*

The plot of a story is given to a child. The child is asked to give as many titles as possible within a few minutes. A score is then given for the total number of titles. For example:

> One day, three friends found a box of gold coins. As they did not want others to know about it, they decided to wait for nightfall before taking the box to a nearby village. One of them went for food and drink, while the other two remained to watch over the gold

and each other. Soon after, they planned to kill their friend when he returned so that each could have more gold coins. The man who went for food and drink wanted all the money for himself, so he put poison in the wine. Upon his return, the two others attacked and killed him. They then ate the food and drank the wine and soon died. No one knows to this day what became of the box of gold coins.

The child gave the following sample titles: "Riches Make Men Bad," "The Lost Treasure," "Gold is Poison," "False Friends," and "Death Wins After All."

### What to Do with It?

This task is very similar to the unusual or alternate uses task used earlier to illustrate the meaning of flexibility. It requires shifts in thinking and has been described by Guilford (1973) as "spontaneous flexibility." It is an ability to produce many different ideas and can aid a person in finding fresh ways of looking at a problem in order to solve it. Ideas that are produced are given credit if they are unusual (that is, if they do not fall in the class of common use). For example:

A pencil is used for writing, but it could also be used as: an arrow, firewood, a pillar for a doll's house, and a toothpick.

### Similar Meanings

The child is required to produce similar meanings for a given word, such as *fun* or *bad*. For example: Let's use the word *fun*. Here are a few words that have a similar meaning: play, frolic, jest, trifling. It calls for the ability to produce alternative relations, and in the adult form it is called "associational fluency." Guilford (1973) observes this kind of ability to be useful in identifying relations in science and in detective work, where seeing relations among alternative solutions for a suitable decision to be made is needed. Acceptable meanings are given credit.

### Writing Sentences

This task deals with the ability to think of alternate ways of organizing basic information. Several words are given and the child is encouraged to write sentences using the words. Each sentence receives credit if it contains a subject and predicate, uses at least two of the assigned words, makes sense, and does not repeat the same organized idea given in the sentence before. For example:

Knife     Dog     Stick     Bone     Dave

The child provided the following sentences:

Dave tied his knife to a pole to make a spear.
The dog crunched the bone.
The lost knife was found by the dog.
Dave flung the bone into the pool.

### Kinds of People

A picture of a commonly known object is given to the child. He is told to write down the kinds of jobs people do that pertain to the object in the picture, such as, for instance, a tree.

The child gave the following responses: lumberjack, forester, botanist, and gardener.

## TORRANCE TESTS OF CREATIVE THINKING

The Torrance Tests of Creative Thinking (1981) measure fluency, flexibility, originality, and elaboration on the figural forms, and the first three of these creative thinking abilities on the verbal forms. The tasks in both the figural and verbal forms are made to be interesting and challenging for children preschool age and up as well as adults. These measures can be given either individually or in groups, depending on age and purpose. For the verbal task, young children dictate their responses to adults, whereas older children write their own responses on test booklets provided to them.

### Verbal Tasks

#### Ask-and-Guess

The first three of the seven tasks that make up the verbal form of the test are named Ask-and-Guess. The tasks allow for the expression of curiosity and assessment of the ability to hypothesize and think of many possibilities. A picture is given to a person who is encouraged to ask questions about what is happening in the picture to guess causes or give reasons for what is taking place, and to guess consequences or the result of the action. Persons taking the test are instructed to give responses that cannot be generated by merely looking at the picture.

#### Product Improvement

Product Improvement is a complex task that allows a person to play with ideas that he or she would not dare to express in a more serious situation. The task encourages the participant to think of the most interesting, unusual, and imaginative ideas to improve a stuffed toy animal to make it more fun for play. Take, for instance, a stuffed dog (Figure 2.9).

A person doing this task is given the following instructions:

> If you would like to find out what kind of thinking is involved in this test, write down as many ways as you can to improve the stuffed toy dog. Give yourself 2½ minutes to do so, though 10 minutes is allowed for this activity in the actual test. Then take a look at the list of common responses at the end of the chapter.

**Figure 2.9**   Improving a Toy Dog. Reprinted
by permission from Khatena, 1978a, p. 36.

### Unusual Uses

The Unusual Uses task is very much like Guilford's Unusual Brick Uses test. A person is asked to think of unusual, interesting, and seldom-thought-of uses of a common object, such as junk cars. The task requires a person to break away from common uses of the object.

A person doing this activity is given the following instructions:

> To find out how well you can do on this task, list as many interesting and unusual uses of junk cars as you can in 2½ minutes. Then look at the list of common responses (a zero score), given at the end of the chapter to check how well you have done.

### Just Suppose

This task is like Guilford's (1973) consequences test and is a variation of the second task of this test, namely, Guess Consequences. The Just Suppose task is designed to elicit a higher degree of fantasy and is expected to work very well with children. A person is asked to think of all the possible things that could take place if something not likely to happen *did* happen. For example, "Just suppose it was raining and all the drops became solid and stood still in the air and didn't move." Each Just Suppose task is accompanied by an interesting drawing depicting the improbable situation.

### Nonverbal Tasks

### Picture Construction

A shape such as a teardrop or jelly bean made of colored paper is given. The test-taker is told to use it as an important part of a picture, with encouragement to add details to give the drawing more meaning. The task is expected to set in motion the tendency toward finding a purpose for something that has definite purpose. Once found, details are to be added to the drawing in such a way that the purpose is achieved. Points are given for originality and elaboration.

### Incomplete Figures

This task is based on the theory that incompleteness of a figure arouses in a person tensions to complete it in the simplest and easiest way possible. Thus, in the act of producing an original picture, a person usually has to control his tensions and delay the joy of completing the picture.

The task consists of 10 incomplete figures accompanied by the following instructions:

> By adding lines to figures on this and the next page you can sketch some interesting objects or pictures. Again, try to think of some picture or object that no one else will think of. Try to make it tell as complete and as interesting a story as you can by adding to and building up your first idea. Make up a title for each of your drawings and write it at the bottom of each block next to the number of the figure.

Here, for instance, are two incomplete figures that can be used according to the instructions given (Figure 2.10).

Points are given for fluency, flexibility, originality, and elaboration. The person doing this task may like to compare the drawings made with the list given at the end of the chapter to see if he or she has gotten away from common or unoriginal responses.

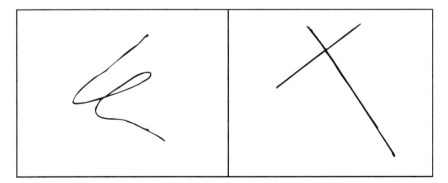

**Figure 2.10**  Completing the Figure to Produce a Picture. Reprinted by permission from Khatena, 1978a, p. 39.

### Repeated Figures

Just like the Incomplete Figures task, the Repeated Figures task gives a person two or three pages of closed figures, such as triangles and lines, with encouragement to use imagination to create pictures using the elements as important parts of them. In theory, the lines are supposed to arouse the creative tendency to bring structure and completeness to what is incomplete, while the triangles require the ability to disrupt or destroy an already complete form.

If a person wishes to have a feel for this kind of thinking, he or she should draw on a sheet of paper six rows of four triangles each. The instructions below are given before the completion of the task, which should be completed in $2\frac{1}{2}$ minutes, though in the actual test 10 minutes is allowed for this activity.

> In $2\frac{1}{2}$ minutes time, see how many objects or pictures you can make from the triangles, the triangles being the main part of whatever you make. With a pencil or crayon, add lines to the triangles to complete your picture. You can place marks inside them, on them, and outside them—whatever you want to do in order to make your picture. Try to think of things that no one else will think of. Make as many different pictures or objects as you can and put as much thought as you can into each one, making them tell a complete and interesting story.

Points are given for fluency, flexibility, originality, and elaboration. Uncommon or original responses are listed at the end of the chapter for the purpose of comparison.

## THINKING CREATIVELY WITH SOUNDS AND WORDS

The two components of the Thinking Creatively with Sounds and Words test (Torrance, Khatena, & Cunnington, 1998) are: 1) Sounds and Images and 2) Onomatopoeia and Images. Both are measures of originality. While Sounds and Images provides sound stimuli, Onomatopoeia and Images provides onomatopoeic word stimuli to the person taking the test. Both measures call for the use of free association in producing original verbal images. These are then scored for originality, based on the principle of statistical infrequency and relevance. The measures invite the use of creative imagination to break away from the obvious and commonplace, created by either sounds or onomatopoeic words to produce original verbal images.

Both components of the test contain helping conditions to facilitate the production of original verbal images. While Sounds and Images presents stimuli in the form of sound sets and Onomatopoeia and Images presents stimuli in the form of onomatopoeic word sets, both have certain built-in conditions to assist the listener in allowing the freedom of imagination to create original images. Both tests provide progressive warm-up, making creative thinking legitimate, provide freedom from the threat of evaluation, invite regression, and aid the breaking of inhibiting sound or word sets.

## Sounds and Images

There are three repetitions of a group of four recorded audio effects in Sounds and Images. The presentation of these sounds are interspersed with narrated instructions that in effect force the listener to reject commonplace associations for freewheeling and imaginative ideas. The test relies upon the principles of the simple to the complex and the common to the unusual to evoke original verbal images.

Each form of the test presents both single and multiple sound sets. Forms 1A and 1B are the children's version of the measure, while Forms 2A and 2B are the adult version of the measure. The first reaction to the presentation of the sounds often results in the production of stereotyped or common responses. Considerable creative power is needed by the participant to break away from the usual sequence of thought into an altogether different pattern of thought, often requiring the power of synthesis, where several sounds must be combined into a thought as a whole, to produce the original.

To get a feel for what the recording does, here is an excerpt of the recorded narrative derived from the Demonstration Record:

> Have you given any thought to the world of sound, that mysterious region just beyond your eardrums? It's as close as the ring of your telephone, the rustle of wind through the trees in your backyard, or the rumble of thunder on a warm summer afternoon.
>
> In just a moment you're going to take a journey into the most fantastic corners of that world…and there hear things you've never heard before. Although the first sound you'll meet along the way should be familiar enough, the others are going to seem somewhat strange to your ears, and you'll most likely scratch your head a bit as you wonder what on earth they might be.
>
> On this journey, you're going to listen to four separate sounds. As you listen to each sound, attempt to picture it in your mind's eye, and then try to write a short description of it on the page before you…
>
> As you listen to the sounds, be sure to use every last bit of imagination you possess while you write down the word pictures they call to your mind. Chances are, the sounds will also call up a host of different feelings within you. Try to capture these feelings as they come to you, and hold onto them until you've written them down. Remember, write down your impressions of each sound as it occurs in the recording…. All set? Here we go, then, into the mysterious world of sound…

## Onomatopoeia and Images

In *Onomatopoeia and Images*, auditory-visual stimuli are presented in the form of onomatopoeic words like "crunch" or "tingle." These words have both sound and meaning elements. Each onomatopoeic word has many layers of meaning, both factual and emotive, established through usage. Onomatopoeic words, when presented to the listener, act as mental sets. They cause the listener at first to think of common meanings of words from which the listener must break away to produce creative responses, This conscious effort involves what Samuel Taylor Coleridge (1817/1956) calls the use of the "secondary imagination" to produce new and unusual response combinations. The sound component of these words subtly strikes the listener unaware, stirring his or her emotions, which lead to thoughts of unusual and imaginative meanings in response to what is heard. The creative process works best to produce original thoughts when both the intellect and emotions are involved.

As in *Sounds and Images*, the test is administered in standard conditions by presenting all instructions on long-playing records or cassette tapes. A narrator prepares the listener by explaining the nature and purpose of the tests and calling him or her to use creative imagination to produce original verbal images. Five onomatopoeic words for the children's version, or Forms 1A and 1B, and 10 onomatopoeic words for the adult version, or Forms 2A and 2B, are read four times. After the first, second, and third readings of the onomatopoeic words, the narrator encourages the listener to use his or her imagination to produce original verbal images.

Here is an excerpt of the recorded narrative derived from the Demonstration Record:

> Do you know that some words are quite musical? You can tell their meanings by their sounds. They can stir your feelings to make you happy or sad, kind or cruel. They can make you behave in a certain way, even when you do not know their meanings.
>
> Musical words seem to have a certain magic, and together with your imagination they can make you think in the way a poet does when he writes a poem or an inventor when he makes something entirely new.
>
> So that you too can show how well you can set your imagination to work, a list of musical words has been given to you. All you have to do is to listen carefully to the words as they are spoken, and by using your creative imagination try to picture in your mind what you think no one else would have thought of. For example, listen to this word "blast." The picture you get at first may be of some kind of explosion, like a bomb explosion, setting off a charge of dynamite, a jet plane taking off, or a volcanic eruption. But anyone could have thought of those. How about you? Listen to the words as they are spoken and each time try to think of a new picture to write about...
>
> Remember to use your imagination to help you think of interesting and unusual pictures to write about. Are you ready?

## CONCLUSION

This chapter has presented several ways that are used to identify creativity. Included are verbal, figural, and auditory measures developed by Guilford, Torrance, and Khatena, respectively. Chapter 3 expands on this by describing other approaches of discovering creative and talented individuals.

## APPENDIX

**List of Common or Unoriginal Responses Scored Zero to Demonstrate Form**

1. Product Improvement (Toy Dog)
   Bark, make it
   Bell, add on neck, feet, etc.
   Bow, add
   Color, add or change
   Cuddly, make it
   Ears, bigger, longer
   Eyes, bigger, move, wink, sparkle, glow, etc.
   Face, give expression personality
   Fluffy, more like real fur
   Fuzzy, make
   Larger, longer, taller, etc.; legs longer
   Mouth, bigger
   Movable parts at joints
   Music box inside
   Noise, have him make
   Nose, bigger
   Paws, add, make bigger, etc.
   Realistic, make
   Ribbon, add brighter color, bigger bow, etc.
   Smile, make
   Softer
   Tail, curl up, make longer
   Tongue, longer

2. Unusual Uses (Junk Cars)
   Art, abstract, modern sculpture, pop art
   Autos, make one from several
   Autos, play on playground
   Chairs
   Demolition derby
   Demonstration, warning for drivers
   Educational uses, rebuild to learn, give to teenagers to learn about cars
   Flower planter
   Playground, pretend cars
   Racing
   Repair to sell
   Scrap iron, metal, etc.

Spare parts, see for use on other cars
Swing, tires used for
Tension reducer, smash with hammer
Tires, recap and sell
Toy on playground

3. Incomplete Figures (Figures in Two Squares)
*Figure in left square:*
Abstract figure
Bird(s)
Human (man, woman, child)
*Figure in right square:*
Horse head or horse body
House
Kite

4. Repeated Figures (Triangles)
Amorphous, indistinct figure
Cottage, house, etc.
Design
Human face
Human figure (man, woman, child)
Star (six point)
Tent, tepee
Tree
Triangle

# 3

## Discovering Creative and Talented Individuals

### OVERVIEW

This chapter discusses the identification of creative and talented individuals. Two measures of creative perceptions, developed by Khatena and Torrance (1998b), and Khatena and Morse (1994), identify creative and talented individuals. In addition, the nature and identification of art talent is discussed, and an art assessment procedure developed by Khatena (1988) is presented.

### INTRODUCTION

We have to this point discussed the measurement of creative process and described a few of the instruments available to identify creative talent in this way. Now let us consider how we may identify creative and talented persons by screening for their individual traits.We give particular focus to persons with talent in art and how we may set out to identify this talent.

### IDENTIFYING CREATIVE PERSONS

According to Mel Rhodes (1961), we can discover creative talent through thinking processes, personality traits, environmental press, and the generation of products. We have discussed a few approaches used to measure creative processing of information, giving particular focus to the measures developed by J. P. Guilford, E. Paul Torrance, and Joe Khatena. Here, we will consider how we may identify creative talent by screening a person's traits, including: personality, intellect, temperament, physique, habits, attitudes, self-concept, value systems, defense mechanisms, and behavior (Rhodes, 1961).

Calvin W. Taylor (1958), well known for organizing several University of Utah Research Conferences on Creativity, and E. Paul Torrance's (1975) 15 years of research on the development of the "Ideal Pupil Checklist," have described some of the most salient intellectual and personality characteristics possessed by creative individuals. Here are some of these characteristics:

- original
- diverse in thought
- good vocabulary
- good brainstorming skills
- detailed
- good problem-solving skills
- inquisitive
- has the ability to reshape things and ideas
- endurance
- observes others
- honest
- curious
- intellectual
- resourceful
- adventurous
- emotionally sensitive
- expressive
- an independent thinker
- industrious
- intuitive or insightful
- likes to work alone
- has many interests
- has perseverance

- playful
- enjoys recognition
- enjoys variety
- enjoys challenge
- open-minded
- enjoys mastering problems
- hungers for knowledge
- likes improving things
- committed
- a nonconformist
- self-sufficient
- independent in judgment
- a risk-taker
- has a good memory
- self-confident
- a sense of beauty
- a good sense of humor
- sincere
- goal-setting skills
- thorough
- a visionary
- prefers complex tasks

Familiarity with such descriptors of the creative person led to the development of a number of instruments for the identification of creative talent. The characteristics that are most viable relate to derivation of information about a person's past either through self-reports or perceptions. The assumption is that past creative behaviors or perceptions can serve as predictors of current and future creative behaviors or perceptions.

Considerable evidence has accumulated to support the use of autobiography as a means of discovering the creative personality (Khatena, 1992; Rimm & Davis, 1980; Schaefer, 1970; Taylor & Ellison, 1966). Instruments that call for information of a person's past may take the form of checklists, questionnaires, or inventories. These have been found to be efficient ways of identifying creative talent.

## Khatena–Torrance Creative Perception Inventory

An inventory battery that serves this purpose effectively is the Khatena–Torrance Creative Perception Inventory (1998b). It consists of two components, each designed in its own right to identify creative individuals. The components are What Kind of Person Are You? and Something about Myself. They are primarily designed for use in measuring creative talent in children from the age of 10 as well as in adults.

### *What Kind Of Person Are You?*
The first component, What Kind of Person Are You?, is based on the rationale that the individual has a psychological self whose structures have incorporated creative and noncreative ways of behaving. The aim of the measure is to present items to trigger those subselves, yielding an index of the individual's disposition or motivation to function in creative ways. The measure contains 50 items of paired characteristics randomly arranged in a forced-choice format. An item may call for the choice between a socially desirable and a socially undesirable characteristic or between a creative and a noncreative characteristic.

The test, designed to measure creative potentials of individuals from 10 years of age to adulthood, is easily administered and takes 10 to 20 minutes to complete. It is also easily interpreted and yields a creative perception index obtained by counting the number of correct responses out of 50, such that 1 point is awarded for each positive response, with scores ranging from 0 to 50. A person taking the test is asked to choose one of each pair, marking it with a ✓ on the answer sheet. Take, for instance, the following two items:

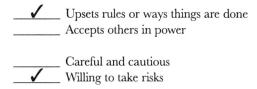

   ✓    Upsets rules or ways things are done
_____ Accepts others in power

_____ Careful and cautious
   ✓    Willing to take risks

In addition to a creative perception index, determined by the total score, What Kind of Person Are You? yields five factors: Acceptance of Authority, Self-confidence, Inquisitiveness, Awareness of Others, and Disciplined Imagination. Scoring keys are provided for the total measure and factor orientations in the test manual.

**Acceptance of Authority.** This factor relates to being obedient, courteous, conforming, and accepting of the judgments of authorities.

**Self-confidence.** This factor relates to being socially well-adjusted, self-confident, energetic, curious, and having a good memory.

**Inquisitiveness.** This factor means always asking questions; being assertive; feeling strong emotions; being talkative; and being obedient.

**Awareness of Others.** This factor relates to being courteous; socially well-adjusted; popular or well-liked; considerate of others; and preferring to work in a group.

**Disciplined Imagination.** This factor is defined as being energetic, persistent, thorough, industrious, imaginative, adventurous, never bored, attempting difficult tasks, and preferring complex tasks.

### Something about Myself

The second component, Something about Myself, is based on the rationale that creativity is reflected in the personality characteristics of individuals, in the kind of thinking strategies they employ, and in the products that emerge as a result of their creative strivings. The aim of the measure is to obtain an index of a person's creativity by the number of positive choices made relative to the items in the three categories of creative functioning.

Something about Myself consists of 50 items or statements. A person taking the test is asked to indicate on the answer sheet whether or not the statement is applicable. The test is easily administered and takes a person 10 to 20 minutes to complete. It is also easily interpreted and yields a creative perception index obtained by counting the number of positive responses out of 50, such that 1 point is awarded for each positive response, with scores ranging from 0 to 50. Take, for instance, the following four items:

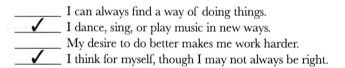

Something about Myself, in addition to a creative perception index, determined by the total score, yields six factors: Environmental Sensitivity, Initiative, Self-strength, Intellectuality, Individuality, and Artistry. Scoring keys are provided for these factor orientations in the test manual.

**Environmental Sensitivity.** This factor involves open-mindedness; sensitivity; relating ideas to what can be seen, touched, or heard; and interest in the beautiful and humorous aspects of experiences.

**Initiative.** This factor relates to directing, producing, or playing the lead in dramatic and musical productions; producing new formulas or new products; and bringing about changes in procedures or organization.

**Self-strength.** This factor is defined as self-confidence in matching talents against others; resourcefulness; versatility; willingness to take risks; the desire to excel; and organizational ability.

**Intellectuality.** This factor relates to intellectual curiosity; enjoying challenge; imagination; preferences for adventure over routine; and a liking for the reconstruction of things and ideas to form something different.

**Individuality.** This factor involves a preference for working by oneself rather than in a group; seeing oneself as a self-starter and somewhat of an eccentric; being critical of others' work; thinking for oneself; and working for long periods without getting tired.

**Artistry.** This factor relates to the production of objects, models, paintings, and carvings; musical compositions; receiving awards or prizes; exibiting work; and the writing of stories, plays, poems, and other literary pieces.

## IDENTIFYING TALENTED PERSONS

The approach to identify creative persons by way of the questionnaire, checklist, and inventory can also be used to discover individuals with many talents. It is based on the same assumption that past behaviors or activities can serve as predictors of current and future talent behaviors. Most often the best way to identify talented individuals is to find a biographical or perception measure that is comprised of multiple scales, each descriptive of a talent area.

Among the several instruments that were constructed for the purpose of identifying multiple talent are the Biographical Inventory Form U (Taylor & Ellison, 1983), and the Gifted and Talented Screening Form (Johnson, 1979). However, perhaps the instrument constructed by Taylor and Ellison is the best researched of these, having taken life from their earlier work on biographical inventories. Biographical Inventory Form U attempts to generate information on talent in the areas of creativity, academic achievement, leadership, and artistic potentials.

### Khatena–Morse Multitalent Perception Inventory

One effective instrument of recent development is the Khatena–Morse Multitalent Perception Inventory (1994). A well designed and researched measure, this test aims at assessing five broad areas of talent of individuals from 10 years of age to adulthood. The instrument generates talent information of individuals in art, music, leadership. creative imagination, and initiative.

The measure comes in alternate forms that can be used to identify talent at all age levels. Each form consists of 50 items and takes an individual 10 to 20 minutes to complete. If the measure is used with children younger than 10 years of age, an adult who knows the person well enough can help in the taking of the test.

The test-taker is asked to indicate on the answer sheet whether or not the statement is applicable. The test is easily administered and interpreted and yields a versatility perception index obtained by counting the number of positive responses out of 50, such that 1 point is awarded for each response, with scores ranging from 0 to 50. Here's an example:

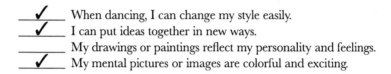

    ✓     When dancing, I can change my style easily.
    ✓     I can put ideas together in new ways.
         My drawings or paintings reflect my personality and feelings.
    ✓     My mental pictures or images are colorful and exciting.

The Khatena–Morse Multitalent Perception Inventory, in addition to a versatility perception index determined by the total score, yields scores for five factors: Artistic, Musical, Creative Imagination, Initiative, and Leadership. Scoring keys are provided for these talent factor orientations in the test manual.

**Artistic.** This factor relates to the expression of ideas, personality, and feelings in interesting and novel ways via art. Items that are included suggest analytic and evaluative skills, in addition to a proficiency in artistic rendition.
**Musical.** This factor includes items that relate to facility in learning and modifying, as well as in singing or playing music or rhythms. Technical skill appears to be a strong component of this factor.
**Creative Imagination.** This factor includes items that emphasize a fluent, vivid imagination, which can be used in accomplishing tasks. The characteristics of uniqueness, resourcefulness, and inquisitiveness are also suggested.
**Initiative.** This factor is defined as items that convey insight, flexibility, and originality in a wide range of endeavor. In addition, self-expression in one's activities are also suggested.
**Leadership.** This factor includes items that emphasize having earned the respect of others, having and understanding effective relationships, and possessing good communicative skills.

The total score on the Khatena–Morse Multitalent Perception Inventory indicates the versatility level of a person, consisting of many areas of talent strength. The factors describe the particular areas of talent strength that a person possesses. For instance, a high score on the artistic factor suggests that a person has a high level of talent in art. The same applies to music, initiative, and leadership. The inventive and innovative component lies with the creative imagination factor. One would expect a person to be creatively talented if the score on creative imagination is high as well.

## THE NATURE AND IDENTIFICATION OF ART TALENT

Ability in the visual arts is more appropriately considered as ability in one or more of the areas in the fine arts. By visual arts we mean drawing, painting, sculpting, designing, and composing art. Abilities required for superior production are not easily measurable, especially in the area of art. That is why we often rely on observable behavior and products of individuals to determine potential talent in visual arts when psychometry cannot help us.

An aspect of importance in art talent is thinking and expressing oneself in the symbolic system unique to art. Just as we use the language of words to express our thoughts, ideas, and feelings to one another, we also use the language of art. As we shall see later in this book, the language of art has its own alphabet, derived from nature and possessed by the artist.

Mental imagery represents the internal and external worlds of an individual and is an important component of thinking and expression in the visual arts. Information from the physical and sociocultural universe reaches the individual through various senses, such as sight, hearing, and touch, to become mental images in the brain. Imagery is said to lie in the nonverbal dimension of the brain. Its role in art is significant because imagery overcomes the barriers of intermediary symbolic systems, like the language of words, to present to the individual visions that eventually find themselves expressed in one art form or another.

Common to all art forms is creativity. It is a processing and energizing agent that differs in degree of operation, depending on the art form used. Regarding creativity and the visual arts, Guilford (1968) focuses attention on the importance of three divergent production abilities in the figural or nonverbal dimension of the structure of intellect: fluency, flexibility, and elaboration. Communication of meaning in the visual arts is done in nonverbal ways and often involves these three divergent thinking operations.

*Fluency* in the figural or nonverbal information area is broken down into *ideational fluency*, or the ability to generate many ideas, and *analogy fluency*, or the ability to organize figural information as systems rapidly.

Two kinds of *flexibility* abilities relate to a shift in thinking from one class of thought to another: *spontaneous flexibility* indicates automatic shifts in thinking; and *adaptive flexibility* indicates shifts in thinking owing to the need for different solutions to a single problem.

Guilford (1968) considers *elaboration* very important to art when, early in a creative production, a general schema, motif, or plan develops that is psychologically a system, to which details are added as the system becomes distinct.

Another ability that has importance and relevance for creative artistic production is the ability to visualize changes in figural information or product transformation, an ability outside divergent thinking, but in the product dimension of "The Structure of Intellect" model.

There is also the ability to evaluate one's own production of an art object. In addition, there is ability in the behavioral category, as this relates to the translation of semantic or behavioral information to figural information.

Victor Lowenfeld and W. L. Brittain (1964) discuss the creative and mental growth of talented children as related to art and identify five major characteristics:

- Fluency of imagination and expression, which relates to ideas that spontaneously flow and imagery that expands with the creative process, as in a chain reaction.
- A highly developed sensibility toward movement, rhythm, content, and organization, such that integration of thinking, feeling, and perceiving is experienced to a high degree by talented individuals.
- An intuitive imagination through which imagery, important to the creative act, is possessed to a high degree by the talented individual.
- Directness of expression, which can be defined as the self-confidence possessed by the talented individual in the act of artistic creation.
- A high level of self-identification with the depicted experience, as exhibited by the talented individual.

Highly specialized knowledge and skill specific to each art form must be acquired by individuals before they can express themselves in the medium of art. Because it takes time for children to acquire this knowledge and skill, it is not unusual to find screening them for art talent potential quite difficult.

There are no completely satisfactory tests of aptitude for art, especially during the school years. Guilford (1968) has described some figural abilities that are important to artistic talent. We have already indicated that these are ideational and expressional fluency, spontaneous and adaptive flexibility, and elaboration, all three in the divergent thinking area of "The Structure of Intellect" model. Guilford suggests that they are measurable in ways relative to the product dimension of "The Structure of Intellect" as follows:

**Figural units.** For example, *Sketches*, which present a simple, basic figure to which is added just enough detail to make a recognizable object: such as a monogram, which requires arrangement of letters to make initials of a name.

**Figural classes.** For instance, *Alternate Letter Groups*, which present a set of capital letters, for example AHVTC, for the formation of subgroups, each of which makes a class that has all straight lines, according to the figural properties of AHVTC.

**Figural systems.** Emphasis is on organization of visual elements into wholes, as for example, the *Making Objects Test*, which requires the use of two or more simple assigned geometric forms to construct a named object.

**Figural transformation.** This is concerned with adaptive flexibility and is in line with the emphasis or shift in thinking. Take, for instance, *Planning Air*

*Maneuvers*, which involves skywriting two capital letters in succession as efficiently as possible, with an airplane pilot being instructed when to start and finish, as well as when to turn the airplane.

**Figural implications.** An instance of this is *Decorations*, where simple outline drawings of common objects, such as a piece of furniture or an article of clothing, are repeated twice, with instructions for filling them in with decorative additions.

These figural abilities have been included and modified in Creativity Tests for Children (Guilford, 1973), which is described in Chapter 2 of this volume. Guilford's measure includes a verbal and nonverbal section, each containing five items. By administering the whole test to students from grades 4 and up, not only will information about an individual's aptitude for talent in art be obtained (figural tasks 6 to 10, namely, Making Something Out of It, Different Groups, Making Objects, Hidden Letters, and Adding Decorations), but also information about his or her creative thinking abilities (using the whole test of 10 tasks).

Another very useful measure for this purpose is the figural forms of the Torrance Tests of Creative Thinking (1981), from which information about figural fluency, flexibility, originality, and elaboration can be derived. All four of these creative thinking abilities are important to art talent, though by themselves they do not necessarily identify a talented student in art.

The figural form of the Torrance Tests of Creative Thinking (1981) comprises three subtests that require students to use their imagination to respond to various assigned shapes and lines, given to each student to produce original pictures. A scoring guide gives scores for fluency, flexibility, originality, and elaboration. Scores derived for these four creative thinking dimensions should tell us about an individual's potential to use creative ways of processing information. However, if the drawings are looked over with care, some indications of art talent may also be observed, although subjects are not asked to meet any artistic standards when producing a picture. Important elements of both creativity and art talent may be identified. It is important to realize that a creativity test is not expected to measure art talent. However, it can indicate that a person with a high creative index on such a test has the potential to process art information and language in imaginative ways, an ability essential to art composition.

There are not many ways to measure specific art ability. Among those that require production of drawings for the purpose of assessing art potential are the Horn Art Aptitude Test (1951) and the Knauber Art Ability Test (1935). The Advanced Placement Program in Studio Art (Dorn, 1976) offers identification of art potential for college placement. The Meier Art Judgment and Meier Aesthetic Perception Test (1940) measure the ability to judge art, but require no exhibition of drawing ability and are consequently of no concern to us here.

**Horn Art Aptitude Inventory** (1951). In brief, this measure, suitable for high school seniors, does not concern itself with advanced skills in art, but rather with predicting future success in artistic activities. It requires students to draw simple pictures, after which they are to compose more elaborate pictures, with a few given lines as clues. The scoring is subjective, but uses various works of quality as criteria.

**Knauber Art Ability Test.** Developed in 1935, this is a much older test. It requires students' actual drawings and rearrangement of pictorial compositions. Responses are scored for quality, according to a key that is provided.

**Advance Placement Program in Studio Art** (Dorn, 1976). This test is designed to appraise the quality of studio art performance by recognizing all the highly subjective elements used in the creation of a work of art. A portfolio—comprised of four original artworks of a specific size as well as several 2 × 2 slides that document other works—is submitted with the help of the students' schools to the Educational Testing Service.

The examination consists of three sections. In Section A, a student's four original compositions of a given dimension are evaluated for quality. In Section B, the student's group of slides that show work over an extended period in an area of concentration is evaluated. In Section C, two slides submitted by the student, each showing proficiency in four broad areas (spatial illusion, drawing, color, and organization of three dimensional materials), are also evaluated.

The judging is done by a number of experts in the field, who rate the components of the portfolio, giving place to uncommon responses in art. All this is done with great care; reliability of evaluations is ensured by the training of the judges before and during their reading of all three sections of the evaluation.

The evaluation of a talented student in studio art performance, although not yet perfect, is considered a step in the right direction for measuring the ability of high school students to benefit from a college education in art.

To identify a talented student in art, some consideration needs to be given to intelligence, as students who are highly talented in art are also generally quite bright; and to talent specific to art, identifiable not only through psychometric tests measuring mental process and personality traits, but also through actual productions. One of the surest ways to spot talented individuals in art is by their productive frequency and level. Talented children are often seen communicating their ideas and feelings nonverbally in their drawings, paintings, and related art forms.

Visual narrative, which is considered a catalyst, or a basic and primary element activating other aspects of artistic talent, is observable in the works of young children (Wilson & Wilson, 1976). The Wilsons cite Alan Garner, Julian Green, and C. S. Lewis as examples of writers who have used visual narrative as children until they were able to use words with sufficient facility to convey the subtlety and complexity of their created worlds. According to them, it is also visual narrative that leads talented children to produce a vast number of drawings, serving as the train engine that pulls with it the freight cars of tension and relief, emotion and feeling, repression and sublimation, symbolization, and expanding aspects of reality.

The educator, involved in the difficult task of identifying art talent, needs to become familiar not only with the personality characteristics and behaviors of talented individuals, but also the creative thinking processes they use in their act of production. The Khatena–Torrance Creative Perception Inventory (1998b) and the Khatena–Morse Multitalent Perception Inventory (1994), used with one or more of the process measures of creativity, such as the figural component of the Torrance Tests of Creative Thinking (1981), should achieve this.

Many other approaches have been suggested by Gilbert A. Clark and Enid Zimmerman (1992), some of which are nominations (open or structured), grades in art courses, review of slides or video presentations, portfolio and performance reviews, interviews, and in-class observations. Consistent with current thoughts, the use of multiple measures for the identification of talent generally and art talent specifically is highly recommended (Clark & Zimmerman, 1992; Khatena, 1992).

Perhaps an assessment procedure for art talent that reflects the preceding discussion may be organized along the lines of the Art Talent Assessment Record (Khatena, 1988) outlined in the Appendix.

## CONCLUSION

This chapter discusses inventory approaches that can be used to discover creative and talented individuals. Such measures were developed by Khatena, Morse, and Torrance, respectively. The nature and identification of art talent also received attention with the presentation of a comprehensive art assessment approach. Chapter 4 deals with the nature of creative imagination and its significance and relevance for art creation.

## APPENDIX: THE ART TALENT ASSESSMENT RECORD*

**1. Figural Abilities (Guilford):**

Fluency
_____ Ideational
_____ Expressional
Flexibility
_____ Spontaneous
_____ Adaptive
Elaboration

**2. Creative or Divergent Thinking:**
a) Creativity Tests for Children (Guilford)

_____ Verbal
_____ Figural

b) Tests of Creative Thinking Figural (Torrance)

_____ Fluency
_____ Flexibility
_____ Originality
_____ Elaboration

**3. Creative Personality Traits:**                  _____ Creative Index
(Khatena & Torrance—KTCPI)
Something About Myself                               _____
What Kind of Person Are You                          _____

**4. Art Achievement:**                     Rating
a) Advanced Placement Program in Studio Art    _____
b) Interview                                   _____

**5. Art Behavior Traits**
_____   Scribbles earlier than most other children.
_____   Produces many ideas in drawings or paintings.
_____   Initiates drawings.
_____   If given a situation, takes it to develop new ones.
_____   Unusual and interesting visual imagery in drawings.
_____   Drawings showing imagery expanding in chain reaction.
_____   Sensitive use of art materials.
_____   Sensitive handling of techniques.
_____   Highly developed sense of movement in drawings.
_____   Highly developed sense of rhythm in drawings.
_____   Great feel for color.
_____   Sensitive to order and organization.
_____   Varies organization of elements to suit different situations.
_____   Interest content.
_____   Tells a story.
_____   Expresses feelings.
_____   Shows confidence when undertaking drawing.
_____   Intense personal identification with experience depicted.
_____   Produces many drawings.
_____   Enjoys expressing self in art.
_____   Likes adding details to a basic idea.
_____   Flexible in use of art materials.
_____   Innovative in selection and use of art materials.
_____   Tends to want to draw unusual situations.
_____   Has unusual ideas for pictures.

*Note:* Information for the inventory may be generated by the teacher, by the pupil reporting about himself or herself, or about someone else the pupil knows; and by the parent.

**6. Multitalent Perception Inventory:**          _____ Art talent
(Khatena & Morse—KMMPI)                          _____ Versatility

**7. Case History:** Collect as much information about the individual from a variety of sources, including direct observation of the individual's art talent exhibited in formal and informal settings.

**8. Information from Other Sources:** Any information derived from anecdotes and observations of parents, teachers, and peers about the behavior of the individual that will give insights on art potential would also be of value.

**9. Summary Assessment:** This is to be based on all the information obtained from the above categories (1–8).

**10. Comments or Remarks:** Direction can be given for the educational placement of individuals showing art talent potential in special programs designed for them.

* Reprinted by permission from Khatena, 1988.

# 4

---

# Art and Creative Imagination

## OVERVIEW

This chapter explores the nature of creative imagination and its significance and relevance to art creation. It begins by describing the characteristics of creativity as applied to art and considers a work to be original using both subjective and objective judgment. The discussion continues, to indicating that information received by the brain is creatively processed to transform it into a work of art. The Creative Imagination Imagery Model is then presented, showing that being creative involves the interactivity of environmental, individual, and cosmic variables.

## INTRODUCTION

We have been told that a work of art is a creative endeavor. Most art teachers at one time or another use the imperative "Be creative!," without really explaining how it may be accomplished. The gap must be bridged between being told to be creative and knowing what needs to be done to show it.

## CREATING ART

When we have a subject, and want to produce a work of art, we have the choice of reproducing as closely as possible what we see before us or what we have in our mind that is the result from previous experience. If we make use of the essentials of either one to produce something new, remote, and clever, the production may be considered original.

To be original is primarily to be creative. In being original, we extend the boundaries to make what we are creating unique. Matthew Arnold (1955), a poet and critic, suggested that we use works of art already acclaimed original as examples, or "touchstones." This is in itself not enough to determine if a work is original or not.

If we were to use a more recent, psychologically based view of what constitutes originality, we will find clever, remote, and statistically infrequent responses to be the main defining criteria (Guilford, 1977). This concept must be coupled with the idea that such elements of originality may refer to what an individual produces relative to the group, or to what an individual produces relative to a personal frame of reference for productivity. Among the most widely used measures of creativity that score original responses of an individual relative to others making up the norm population are the Torrance Tests of Creative Thinking (1981) and the Thinking Creatively with Sounds and Words test (Khatena & Torrance, 1998a). A measure of originality designed especially for preschool children is the Shapes Test (Starkweather, 1971). In this test, 10 shapes are presented four times to a child. A response by this child is original if it is not repetitive. In either method, numerical values for originality are given. On their own, such approaches may be insufficient to determine the originality of a work, although they are widely used.

Guidelines need to be established that take into account both known subjective judgment and open-minded objective possibilities. It is helpful to know what went on in the past as we stand at the forefront, prepared to break new ground. The "touchstone" approach relates to the development of taste for the beautiful, while the psychological approach emphasizes infinite possibilities for the original.

Art involves the transformation of endless varieties of extrinsic (or outer) and intrinsic (or inner) information sources into something "rich and strange." This is to say that information is not only obtained from sources around us through our senses, but also from sources that are ideational and of the mind, combined in new or magical ways to bring about transformations.

## CREATIVE PROCESSING OF INFORMATION

What, we may ask, produces transformation? In *nature*, transformation occurs through the process of evolution, which advances as a result of mutation and hybridization. There are numerous examples of transformations to be observed in the physical laboratory of nature, for instance, the caterpillar changing to a moth or butterfly, the tadpole to a frog, the seed to a plant, and water to ice.

In the *laboratory of the human mind*, transformation is brought about by mental activity or intellectual processing. The capacity to effect transformation is largely inherited, but experiences expand to greater functional heights through its interaction with the environment and its consequent use. Such capabilities are also known as abilities that may be organized to take different processing forms. A few of the most potent forms include the mental evolutionary process of establishing order, its dismemberment and reordering to produce a higher order (Land, 1973), which can be labeled as the process of synthesis-destructuring-restructuring; and metaphorical-analogical thinking and creative problem solving, of which incubation and illumination are essential functions (Khatena, 1984, 1992, 1995).

Information is received at first through the *senses* via neurophysiological pathways of the body (for example, sight, hearing, and touch) and registered in the brain as *images*. These images are then labeled in one *language* form or another or in more than one language form. Among the most commonly known label systems used are the verbal, numerical, and musical alphabets. To this must be added the *alphabet of visual art*, which is the basis of all art composition and communication. For instance, information that reaches the artist is not only labeled or coded in the *language of visual art*, but may be simultaneously labeled or coded in the *verbal language* form as well.

The *intellect* processes information in the form of images or their language labels, or both. Such information for processing may be the result of fresh sensory input (for example, an apple, a whistle, and sandpaper) in the form of images or previously processed input that finds expression in language. The interactive nature of images and their language referents in adults negate obvious separation of the two. With very young children, it is different, for prior to language communication, children are at first totally dependent on image information and its processing for understanding and dealing with their world.

The artist, in the act of producing the new, often relies on information from the internal (that is, mentally stored) or from the external (that is, physical and sociocultural) environment. This information is processed by intellectual resources organized to reproduce the representative kind or to produce the imaginative kind. In either case, the artist is in control, such that unique and original products result. In rare instances, artists may implore and receive influences that are beyond their control to assist them in the creative shaping of a work of art. The source of these influences are cosmic. They are known by various names, such as the muses, God, and divine vibrations. Intuited by artists, these influences provide the inspiration and energy that direct artistic creation.

## CREATIVE IMAGINATION IMAGERY MODEL

A theoretical model that illustrates the previous discussion is the Multidimensional Interactive Creative Imagination Imagery Model (Khatena, 1984, 1992, 1995). The model (see Figure 4.1) comprises three dimensions, two of which are the *Environment* and the *Individual*, are mainly used in creative imagination activity. The third, occurring in rare instances, refers to the *Cosmic*.

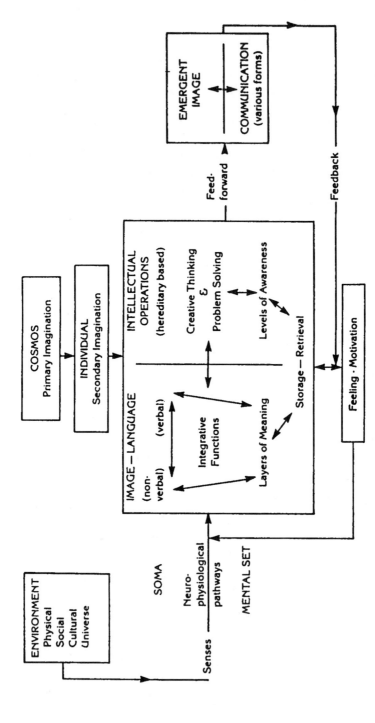

**Figure 4.1** The Multidimensional Interactve Creative Imagination Imagery Model. Reprinted by permission from Khatena, 1984.

## Environment

Everything external to a person constitutes the *Environment*. This dimension includes all that is of the physical universe (plants, trees, animals, birds, insects, earth, mountains, clouds, stars, human beings, and so on) and, as it relates to people either as individuals or groups, the sociocultural universe.

The *natural environment* also includes man-made extensions of it by way of buildings, bridges, products of an advancing technology, clothing, artifacts, and so on. Artists, like everyone else, observe and assimilate all that is in the environment, which provides the informational base used by them to create all kinds of art.

The *sociocultural environment* is comprised of human beings who have developed unique ways of thinking, feeling, speaking, and living that have evolved into complex behavior patterns and rituals identified as culture. Ruth Benedict (1935), a well-known cultural anthropologist, provides confirmation of this when she observes that an individual not only is shaped by culture, but also by living with others as a. As such, the sociocultural environment affects the individual growing up.

Cultural shaping spread over time is developmental. Its influence gradually impinges upon the individual developmentally, shaping intellect and creativity, as it does the rest of the personality. That is why individual development cannot be considered as isolated from its sociocultural origins.

Two scholars, Silvano Arieti (1976) and Dean K. Simonton (1978), have seriously investigated the effects of culture on individuals. The crucial question asked was why creative geniuses appear at a certain time or place and not at another. They concluded that such occurrences happen in clusters finding reason for this in special sociocultural events that affect the development of creative geniuses.

According to Simonton's (1978) historical analyses of eminent men like Aristotle, Michelangelo, Shakespeare, and Beethoven, certain conditions facilitate or hinder the emergence of creative giants. He was led to make a critical distinction between sociocultural events influencing a creator's productivity (for example, constant warfare and its aversive impact on a person's output at a certain time in his career) and sociocultural events influencing a creator's developmental period (for example, formal education, role models for emulation, and their facilitative or hindering influences). Of the two, the latter is far more important to the emergence of eminence.

Other sociocultural events that may affect a creator's productivity include the spirit of the times, or *zeitgeist*, political fragmentation, civil disturbances, and political instability. Simonton (1978) concludes that the significance of sociocultural conditions on creative development not only explain the rarity of eminence in our times, but also direct our attention to those shaping influences in our society that facilitate or hinder creative development during the formative years of the young growing up.

We find further support from Arieti (1976) on the significance of culture in shaping the creativity of geniuses. According to him, individual possibility for genius is more frequent than the occurrence of genius. Furthermore, he states that potentiality for creativity exists in everyone and that it can be cultivated.

Arieti (1976) calls cultures that promote creativity "creativogenic." According to him, potentially creative persons and creativogenic cultures are two essential facets of creativity. Individuals make about two contacts with culture. The first relates to an individual's use of biological equipment to understand the environment and to satisfy needs, and the second relates to an individual's acquisition of things already present in the culture mediated by interpersonal relationships.

Arieti (1976) perceives the individual and culture as open systems, such that the individual both gives to culture and takes from it. A creativogenic society makes available to an individual creative elements seen or accepted as similarly existing in the individual. In this way, preparation is made for a *magic synthesis* of both facets for innovation that becomes a part of culture. Accordingly, a creativogenic society offers an individual the possibility of becoming great without making the occurrence of greatness automatic.

Several conditions present in a creativogenic society are expected to facilitate greatness. These are identified by Arieti (1976) as the availability of cultural means (that is, an elite to preserve these cultural means; the accessibility to equipment, materials, etc.); and openness to cultural stimuli (that is, cultural stimuli are present, requested, desired, and made easily available). Other facilitative conditions relate to the emphasis on becoming and not just being, as well as free access to cultural media for all without discrimination. Freedom or even retention of moderate discrimination after severe oppression or absolute exclusion is to be regarded as an incentive to creativity. Furthermore, additional facilitative conditions include exposure to different and even contrasting cultural stimuli; tolerance for, and interest in, diverging views; interaction of significant persons; and promotion of incentives and rewards.

## Individual

The *Individual* dimension concerns itself with the physical makeup of individuals (for example, eyes, ears, nose, tongue) through which information from the world around reaches them. It also relates to the mental or psychological makeup of people, whereby information in its original or natural form (for example, plants, birds, stars, rivers) from the environment or in its human-processed form (for example, written or spoken language, art, music, mathematics) reaches them. Such information is then transmitted or sent to the brain via neurophysiological pathways. The original or raw form of information is recorded in the brain as images. Information as images are then processed in language form (that is, through an alphabet of words, numbers, music, or art). This means that raw information or experiences are symbolized for ease of mental processing. Storage of information occurs in the dual image-language form, to be retrieved when needed in either or both forms.

Not all information is accepted for recording in the brain. Some of it is rejected and some is perceptually modified by a filter system we call *mental set.* This filter system is established by past experiences for the survival of the individual. It prepares the way for the "assimilation" and "accommodation" of new information to expand the existing informational base, thereby providing even greater opportunities for more effective intellectual functioning.

In this way, an individual's external reality of the physical and sociocultural universe is internalized to become the private world of the individual. It is a reality that provides informational content for *intellectual processing* and determines those influences that control an individual's mental life and behavior.

As for mental processing capabilities, the individual has *hereditary-based intellectual operations* that can be organized in different ways. These abilities help us to understand, remember, think, and judge all information and experience, and in so doing give meaning to our lives. They are the basis not only for survival activity but also for creative endeavors. Processing information for creative purposes brings about the organization of creative thinking abilities for problem solving, for synthesizing-destructuring-restructuring, for analogical-metaphorical thinking, and for overall functioning of the creative imagination.

Other aspects of the *Individual* dimension include several levels of awareness. These are the *conscious, preconscious,* and *unconscious,* terms that Sigmund Freud (1923/1957) used to describe an individual's mental life. The *conscious* relates to current awareness of occurrences or events around us, and can be associated with the state of wakefulness. Carl Jung (1921) considered the *unconscious* as personal or collective. The *personal unconscious* consists of dimmed memories and repressed materials, whereas the *collective unconscious* consists of the patterning of the brain comprehensible only through myths, metaphors, and symbols of dreams, world culture, and religion. The *preconscious* is an area of awareness that is accessible to the conscious, which draws its materials from the *unconscious.*

Harry Stack Sullivan (1953) explains these three areas of our mental life as "good me," "not-me," and "bad-me." "Good-me" is defined as a full awareness or consciousness related to one's positive self-concept, where one's intellectual operations are in full command of informational input to the brain. "Not-me," or the *preconscious,* is that area of mental life where frightening and uncanny experiences, such as those encountered in dreams or nightmares, occur. "Bad-me," or the *unconscious,* is where images or ideas that cause pain, anxiety, or guilt are stored, beyond our consciousness or repressed in defense of the self or ego. These remain active and cause some of the behaviors that occur when our defenses are relaxed, such as when we are dreaming, when we have a slip of the tongue, or are under the influence of alcohol or drugs.

The *preconscious,* according to John Curtis Gowan (1974), is the source of our creativity. It can be strengthened, protected, and enlarged through regular use and increased mental health. Development of the preconscious and its relationship between the conscious and unconscious states of mind are illustrated in Figure 4.2.

When creative persons use *intuition* to access the *preconscious,* leaks occur through the permeable membrane separating it from the *unconscious,* as it were, by osmosis. Often this activity manifests itself in various works of art, for unlike the scientist who

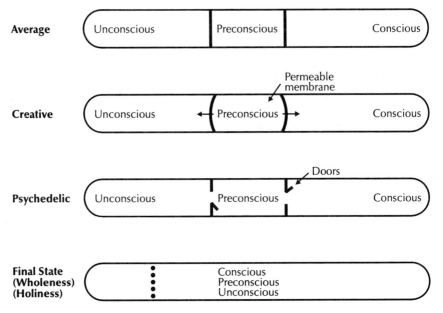

**Figure 4.2**  Development of the Preconscious. Reprinted by permission from Gowan, 1974, p. 83.

depends more on disciplined imagination and the cognitive processes, the artist relies much more on intuition and the secondary imagination for his or her creativity.

Psychedelia, or state-of-mind expansion, occurring naturally without drug assistance is a higher level of the *preconscious*. In a psychedelic state, the barriers separating the *conscious* from the *unconscious* may be thought of as doors that swing open to admit resources of the *preconscious* for intellectual processing leading to productive consequences. The three levels of consciousness become integrated into one, as the barriers that separate them completely disappear and a state of wholeness or holiness emerge.

The *preconscious* can be accessed either by *intuition* or *training*. Creativity that is *intuitive* prepares a person for *psychedelic creativity* when resources of the *preconscious* become available not so much by chance, but by will. In an analogy, Gowan (1978) compares the *training* of the *preconscious* to the taming of a colt by a young child:

> At first the child is afraid of the horse [colt] and cannot ride him; the horse is skittish, unbroken and unpredictable. Eventually through many intermediary stages, the child learns to ride the horse and the horse is taught to accept the rider, until finally the man is complete master of the animal, now fully amenable to his commands. (p. 219)

The highest level of creative processing of information for transformation involves intuition, intellectual activity of analogy and metaphor, emotive-motivational states, the *preconscious*, and several levels of awareness. These function in an integrative way in the act of *creative imagination*, which Samuel Taylor Coleridge (1956) called the "secondary imagination."

Closely linked to the creative springs of mental functioning is the act of *communication*, by which the private activity and experiences of the intellect are made manifest to others. Communication may take various language forms. For the artist, it is the *figural alphabet* that communicates thoughts, feelings, and experiences of the private world of art. When communication has occurred, information received by others evoke reactions that activate the feedforward-feedback loop for continued functioning of all dimensions of the model. Just as information received as images is codified in *visual language* form, and sometimes simultaneously codified in *verbal language* form, so too in the communication stage, processed information may not only manifest itself as *visual art*, but also in the form of *verbal* expression. This end result will then serve as further input information for further individual processing.

## Cosmic

We now come to the third dimension of the model known as the *Cosmic*. The original creative life force, the *Cosmic* is the power and action manifested in all that is or exists; it is the grand source of creativity. Products are but specific instances of it. The *Cosmic* is the parent of *inspiration in the highest sense*. Geniuses in the arts and sciences have testified to its necessity to the creation of their great works.

Poets and artists of ancient Greece, for instance, invoked the Muses to inspire them to great composition. The Romantic poets identified this power as "imagination. William Blake called it "spiritual energy," William Wordsworth refers to it as "absolute power," and Samuel Taylor Coleridge considers it an "ability of prime importance" (cited in Bowra, 1969). According to Coleridge (1956), creative acts of human beings are merely microcosmic simulations of the creative act of God whose . power, "primary imagination," may filter into Man as "secondary imagination."

For Johannes Brahams, inspiration is of divine origin, felt as awe-inspiring vibrations, thrilling his whole being, impelling him to compose his music:

> I begin by appealing directly to my Maker…I immediately feel vibrations which thrill my whole being…In this exalted state I see clearly what is obscure in my ordinary moods: then I feel capable of drawing inspiration from above as Beethoven did. (cited in Abell, 1964, pp. 19–21)

Puccini indicated that the music of his opera *Madame Butterfly* was dictated to him by God. Whereas, Richard Wagner, a German composer, felt himself to be one with this force he calls *vibrations*. *Vibrations*, felt in altered states of consciousness, suggest a *resonance* effect, observable in the sympathetic vibrations of an untensed snare of a drum to a string on a double base. Resonance occurring between two tuning forks is another example of this, where the molecular structure, shape, and size of the tuning forks is such that they produce the same frequency of sound when struck. This means that when one fork is struck, it elicits a similar vibration from the other.

A recent provocative speculation of Man's relation with the universe is Pribram-Bohm's hologram model of ultimate reality. This model draws from the holographic invention of Dennis Gabor, a Nobel Laureate in 1971, created by an interference pattern on a photographic plate. According to this technique, light from one of two laser beams, or the referent beam, directly reaches the photographic plate. At the same time, light from the second laser beam on an object is deflected by a mirror to the photographic plate, producing a three-dimensional representation of the object. This representation is called a *hologram*.

Hamdon-Turner (1981) illustrates this process analogically. The author indicates that if two pebbles were thrown into a pan of water, each would generate concentric ripples that in combination form an interference pattern. If at this point in time the surface is quickly frozen and a laser light is made to shine through it, a holographic image of the two stones is recreated. This means that the images of the stones are encoded in every part of the rippled ice, such that they can be recreated from any part of it.

An interpretation of this analogy in terms of individual-cosmic relations, given in an earlier work (Khatena, 1984), was presented as follows:

> In the first instance, the laser beam shining upon the object whose light is then deflected upon the photographic plate, is analogous to the illumination of information in the human brain through its non-operations as a copy of its universal or ideal form. The direct or reference beam reaching the plate direct is analogous to the cosmic illumination of the ordinary. In the brain, the synergistic function of both creates the hologram that is at one and the same time human and cosmic reality become unified. In the second instance, the concentric ripples may be said to represent the signals of the copy sent out by the mind to meet signals of its generic universal to be illuminated by cosmic energy for transformation to occur, whereby both the copy and universal are one reality. In essence cosmic activity unifies specific and general activity to give us glimpses of ultimate reality. (p. 59)

This is also the case for personal and transpersonal consciousness, where the resonance between the holographic structure of the brain and that of the universe arises from structural similarity. This allows for the transference of information from implicate to explicate order, entirely encoded through the implicate, thereby providing consciousness with access to all knowledge (Gowan, 1980).

In short, human creative energy is the microcosmic projection of the *Cosmic*, whose force sets in motion the wonder of creative imagination that transforms the real world into the magic kingdoms of scientific discovery, invention, and art.

## CONCLUSION

In this chapter, we have given attention to creative imagination and the role it serves in art expression. Creative imagination can be thought of as an information-processing vehicle to bring about transformation. In addition, a multidimensional model of imagery and creative imagination is presented. The model comprises three major interactive components that are involved in creativity: Environment, Individual, and Cosmic. The next chapter expands this discussion to include imagination as derived from divine influences, individual intuition, and thinking.

# 5

## Related Dimensions of Creative Imagination

### OVERVIEW

This chapter expands the discussion of the multidimensional nature of imagery and creative imagination to include its divine origins and relationship to individual intuition and thinking. Creative imagination as constructive fantasy and testimonies of creative geniuses showing creative acts inspired by cosmic or divine influences are presented. In addition, this chapter discusses the intuitive and thinking nature of creative imagination.

### INTRODUCTION

Of all human mental faculties, the creative imagination is the most wondrous. It is the power of mind that distinguishes the fundamentals of things to empower relationships among them for the birth of the new. Creative imagination is constructive fantasy, which transforms reality into dreams and dreams into reality.

### CREATIVE IMAGINATION AS CONSTRUCTIVE FANTASY

In *Romeo and Juliet*, William Shakespeare has Mercutio explain that our imaginative fantasies are created by Queen Mab, the Fairies' midwife, who gallops over men's noses as they lie asleep at night.

In *A Midsummer Night's Dream*, Shakespeare distinguishes the imagination of the lunatic, lover, and poet:

> The lunatic, the lover and the poet
> Are of imagination all compact:
> One sees more devils than vast hell can hold,
> That is, the madman: the lover, all as frantic,
> Sees Helen's beauty in a brow of Egypt:
> The poet's eye, in a fine frenzy rolling,
> Doth glance from heaven to earth, from earth to heaven;
> And as imagination bodies forth
> The forms of things unknown, the poet's pen
> Turns them to shapes and gives to airy nothing
> A local habitation and a name. (V.i.7–17)

Like the poet, the artist is a dreamer, a realist, and a craftsman, who takes elements of the real world to consciously manipulate and combine them by the force of creative imagination into a work of art (Preble, 1973). In the act of creative imagination, a person experiences a sameness in difference, such that opposites become one and person and content find identity in each other in transcendental unity (Durr, 1970).

The many faces of creative imagination include *cosmic* or divine influence, *intuition*, and *thinking*. At this point, the reader should refer to Figure 4.1, noting its *cosmic* and *individual* dimensions. Both of these may be involved in the processing of informational input as images or their language referents.

## Cosmic or Divine Influence

The Romantic poets and those who immediately followed, more than others before them, provided a compendium of various facets of the creative imagination related to psychedelic and aesthetic experience (Durr, 1970). Samuel Taylor Coleridge, William Wordsworth, and William Blake were perhaps the most aware of the metaphysical profundities, and their psychological and philosophical implications. As indicated in Chapter 4, they deified the source of imagination, calling it "spiritual energy," "absolute power," "Reason in her most exalted mood," and "an ability of prime importance."

In *Tintern Abbey*, composed in 1798, Wordsworth (1988) describes the omnipresence of imagination and the oneness he experiences with it:

> ...And I have felt
> A presence that disturbs me with the joy
> Of elevated thoughts; a sense sublime
> Of something far more deeply interfused,
> Whose dwelling is the light of setting suns,
> And the round ocean and the living air,

And the blue sky, and in the minds of man;
A motion and a spirit, that impels
All thinking things, all objects of all thoughts. (lines 93–102)

Samuel Taylor Coleridge (1956) considered imagination as *primary* and *secondary*. *Primary imagination* was to him the "living Power and prime Agent of all human Perception … a repetition in the finite mind of the eternal act of creation in the infinite I AM" (p. 167). An echo of it is the *secondary imagination*, "co-existing with the conscious will, yet identical with the primary," and through whose creative activity is reflected and expressed the infinite: it "dissolves, diffuses, dissipates, in order to recreate, or where this process is rendered impossible…it struggles to idealize and to unify" (p. 167). The imaginative man is a creator through whom God creates and knows and loves (Durr, 1970).

We have already referred to Johannes Brahams's deific attribution to inspiration prior to musical composition. Invoking divinity prior to the urge to compose results in feelings of vibrations that put him in touch with the Maker. A semi-trancelike state follows when the vibrations take the form of distinct mental images that precipitate the flow of ideas, giving birth to musical composition:

> Straightaway the ideas flow in upon me directly from God, and not only do I see distinct themes in the mind's eye, but they are clothed in the right forms, harmonies, and orchestration. Measure by measure the finished product is revealed to me when I am in those rare, inspired moods. (cited in Abell, 1964, pp. 19–21)

John Curtis Gowan (1977) identifies three phases in the process of high creativity in musical composers:

1. the prelude ritual, conscious or unconscious, often ending with an invocation;
2. an altered state of consciousness or creative spell, when the creative idea is born, starting with vibrations followed by mental images and a flow of ideas finally clothed in musical form; and
3. the postlude, where positive emotions about the experience suffuse the participant.

According to Gowan (1980), the composer experiencing vibrations can be said to be "in tune with the Infinite," much like a "radio receiver, when tuned to the exact wavelength of the sending station, can amplify and recover sound made miles away" (p. 283). However, let us note that the recipient of these signals is not necessarily passively awaiting them, but is also, perhaps without full awareness, transmitting signals. It seems that the dynamic meeting of creative cosmic energy beaming into human consciousness becomes the catalyst of specific creative expression.

Already described in Chapter 4 is a recent speculation on the relation of Man and the Universe that includes the Pribram-Bohm hologram theory of ultimate reality. To this must be added J. White and Stanley Krippner's (1977) association of the cosmic dimension of creative imagination with the *psi* phenomenon. However, they avoid explaining *psi* as supernatural in origin, rather as psychic energy emergent from the individual and group, transcending ordinary time, space, and force constraints.

From another source (Krishna, 1977) comes the explanation that psychic energy emerges from bioenergy (*prana*) with psychic energy being "the life force in humans which drives evolution and leads the race in a higher state of consciousness (*kundalini*)" (p. 84). Cosmic energy, a derivative of bioenergy, is an omnipresent, intelligent force that transforms into psychic energy, becoming fuel for an individual's thought, for both "mind and thought are forms of a cosmic energy."

## Intuitive Imagination

Intuitive imagination, closely allied to primary imagination, provides the link between cosmic energy and human creativity. It closely resembles secondary imagination. The source of power of secondary imagination is with the Infinite, but its activity to create finite.

Intuition, defined by *Webster's* (1980) as "instantaneous apprehension" or the "immediate knowing or learning of something without the conscious use of reasoning," is acted upon by creative imagination to produce the new and the beautiful. It serves as a key to many an artist attempting to unlock nature's treasures.

Zoa Rockenstein (1989) sees intuition as an open channel to universal sources of knowledge and wisdom that transcends the boundaries of time, space, the senses, and the logical-rational mind. It comes as an insightful flash or illumination to pattern information and understanding as wholes, much like Graham Wallas's (1926) incubation-illumination stages in the problem-solving process.

Intuition, relative to a treatise on creative design in art, according to Adolf Best-Maugard (1926/1952), contrary to *Webster's* definition, does not mean unconscious, emotional, or instinctive reaction, but conscious-free action. He operationalizes intuition as the comprehension of emotional feeling through which one arrives at a direct comprehension of harmony of the universe.

> This comes through self-development...which brings with it the power of acting freely within the laws, of being to a certain extent in harmony with the universe. Knowledge gives a larger field to our receptivity, making the universe more accessible and bringing us closer to reality. (p.166–167)

We have testimonies of writers, musicians, artists, and scientists explaining that peak experiences are the intuitive phenomenon of creativity. Intuitive imagination does not occur on its own, but operates in a holistic and interactive framework of human-cosmic functioning. It is sometimes attributed to the individual and sometimes to the individual activated by cosmic-deified energies, visions, vibrations, and inspirations, which are subject to self-development.

**Thinking Imagination**

According to John Eccles (1958/1972), creative imagination is the most profound of human activities, generating new insights and illuminations. At the physiological level, the brain must have a sufficient number of neurons, which have a wealth of synaptic connections and the sensitivity to maintain considerable memory patterns, or engrams, through usage. To exhibit creative imagination, such a brain must have the unique capacity for unresting activity that continually combines and recombines these engrams in new ways.

Eccles (1958/1972) attributes creative brain functioning to the right cerebral hemisphere. Its processing is spatial, holistic, simultaneous in nature, and capable of handling complex information. Although both the right and left hemispheres of the brain are integrative in function, the right brain specializes in the handling of divergent and insightful thinking, invention, and production of analogy and metaphor in the service of creative imagination. The left brain is known to specialize in the handling of incoming perceptual information and its language referents, using the logical-analytic thought and decision modes in a continuous stream of conscious internal discourse.

Psychologically, creative imagination requires thinking that can be broadly defined, in terms of "The Structure of Intellect" model, as mental operations that involve cognition, memory, convergent and divergent thinking, and evaluation (Guilford, 1977). These mental operations can be organized in several ways, depending upon how information and mind events are to be processed. Most pertinent of these are processes associated with the forming of an order, breaking it to establish a new order at a higher level to effect transformation; making analogy and metaphor to create original relationships; and creative problem solving involving preparation, incubation, illumination, and verification. All of these are facets of what Samuel Taylor Coleridge (1956) has called the "secondary imagination," which anticipates recent definitions of imagination as mind action aimed at producing new ideas and insights, or generating new hypotheses for problem solving.

Creative imagination, according to R. W. Gerard (cited in Ghiselin, 1955) is "an action of mind that produces a new idea or insight" (p. 226) or "the heat of mental work transforming the soft ingot of fancy into the hard steel of finished creations" (p. 227).

C. M. Bowra (1969) explains imagination as problem-solving activity aimed at producing ideas and insightful solutions, such that "when we use our imagination we are first stirred by some alluring puzzle which calls for a solution, and then by our own creations in mind, we are able to see much that was before dark or unintelligible" (p. 7).

For Peter McKellar (1957), thinking is of two kinds: one he calls "R-Thinking," which relates to reasoning, logic, and reality-adjustment, and the other is "A-Thinking," which relates to dreaming, fantasy, and mental events prominent in psychosis, and the creative process and act. It is A-Thinking that he calls imagination.

Apart from having properties similar to Wallas's (1926) problem-solving paradigm, creative imagination, according to Harold Rugg (1963), incorporates feeling and logical thinking moods with the transliminal mind, where lives all human experience and where in the absence of free censorship illumination occurs.

Growth is the key concept of George Land's (1973) transformation theory, which deals with the evolutionary properties of establishing order and its dismemberment for the formation of a new and higher order. In terms of creative imagination, his theory can be explained as the process of synthesis-destructuring-restructuring for the purpose of bringing about recurring new transformations. This process involves the selection of certain kinds of information to the exclusion of others. Items chosen are ordered or synthesized to create a structure that hitherto did not exist. A time comes when dissatisfaction with this order precipitates change. The structure is ready to be pulled apart into its primary elements, to be reorganized or restructured in a new and more elegant form, at which time transformation is said to have occurred.

Creative thinking, involved in imagination, can be organized to produce analogies and metaphors. These are constructed by the creative intellect to be communicated in direct visual, auditory, or kinesthetic forms through art, music, and dance, respectively. Indirect communication by analogy and metaphor occurs via verbal, quantitative, figural, or other language forms (such as poetry, drama, art, physics, or chemistry). The form of communication chosen will vary from one individual to another, depending on the use of or familiarity with language or non-language systems.

## CONCLUSION

Related dimensions of creative imagination are discussed in this chapter. Their roots, according to testimonies of creative geniuses engaged in creative acts, lie in inspiration received from the cosmic or divine. Other facets of imagination involved in creativity are intuition and thinking. Chapter 6 explores the subject of imagery as the language of discovery. It also deals with art in the visual mode as possessing a language of its own.

# 6

## Imagery as Language of Discovery

### OVERVIEW

This chapter describes the nature of imagery and deals with imagery as the language of discovery. Art in the visual mode of imagery possesses a language all its own, in the form of seven generic figural motifs. These are structured and processed in various ways by creative imagination to produce beautiful and original works of art.

### INTRODUCTION

Often, we do not realize that information about the world does not reach us at first as language, but as images. Whereas language is the symbolic form of information and is man-made, images are primarily brain recordings of environmental information and is acquired through the senses and nervous system. They occur in the absence of the objects represented. As such, images are unlikely to be exact copies of the objects they represent, for information received as images are mediated and modified by a filtering system determined by prior experiences and feelings (see Figure 4.1)

## THE NATURE OF IMAGERY

Images as informational input are not only visual (seeing), but also auditory (hearing), tactile (touching), kinesthetic (moving), olfactory (smelling), gustatory (tasting), and organic (body sensations). Such input is often multisensory and interactive. Information, in the form of objects and events (for example, a mental image of an ant walking on the icing of a cake) first internalized as images, constitute first-order representations of the environment. Language follows images; it provides culture-specific labels to images to become second-order representations, as in the words *cockroach* or *scorpion*, which stand for the actual insects. Image and language experiences are both stored in memory to serve as content for processing by the intellect and creative imagination (see Figure 4.1).

Images are private to the individual and have a life of their own. They are set to work by creative mental processes organized in several ways to effect transformation by creativity. As images interact with an individual's mental-emotive life or psyche, they may integrate as imagery to represent the individual's life patterns, character, thinking style, behavior, and general nature. A good example of this is to be found in William Shakespeare's play *Othello*, where the overthrow of Othello's mind by Iago is illustrated by imagery exchange. At the beginning of the play, Othello uses high-minded images (universe, monumental alabaster, adamantine chains), whereas Iago uses sewer-like images (for example, two-backed beast, the spider in the cup). As the play develops, Iago convinces Othello that Desdemona, his wife, is unfaithful. The turning point comes when Othello, totally consumed with jealousy and believing in the infidelity of his wife, uses Iago's images, while Iago uses Othello's images.

Imagery is both private and universal, unique to the individual yet common to all humanity. It belongs to the individual, but, shaped by the physical and sociocultural world, is rooted to culture, civilization, and the cosmic order.

## DISCOVERY BY IMAGERY

Imagery and its language referents have much to do with creative imagination. John Eccles (1958/1972) explains that by association, the image is evocative of other images. When these beautiful and subtle images blend in harmony and are expressed verbally, pictorially, and musically, for instance, they evoke transcendent experiences in others. They become the occasion of artistic creation of a simple or lyrical kind. If they occur in the problem-solving mode, illumination and new insight may result. In science, the image may take the form of a new hypothesis that transcends an earlier one.

Many creative geniuses have testified that, in their acts of composition and invention, imagery served them as the vehicle for discovery. By its nature, imagery, relatively least affected by cultural constraints, is more fluid and malleable to creative processing than its language correlate.

Albert Einstein, for instance, tells us that in the creative mode of thinking, images, primarily visual and motor, rather than words or language, served him as elements of thought. The logic of language only served to communicate his illuminations.

The words or the language, as they are written or spoken do not seem to play any role in my mechanism of thought. The psychical entities which seem to serve as elements in thought are certain signs and more or less clear images which can be voluntarily reproduced and combined...this combinatory play seems to be the essential feature in productive thought—before there is any connection with logical construction in words or other kinds of signs which can be communicated to others...the above mentioned elements are, in my case visual and some of muscular type. Conventional words or other signs have to be sought for laboriously only in the secondary stage, when the mentioned associative play is sufficiently established and can be reproduced at will. (cited in Ghiselin, 1955, p. 43)

Other scientific discoveries, such as the principle of the rotating magnetic field (Nikola Tesla) and the structure of the carbon ring (Friedrich Kekule von Stradonitz), were precipitated by imagery. The composition of *Kubla Khan* was the result of Samuel Taylor Coleridge's experiencing images while in a dream state. Wolfgang Amadeus Mozart and Johannes Brahams have both indicated the significance of imagery to their musical inspiration and composition.

In his poem, *I Wandered Lonely as a Cloud*, composed in 1804, William Wordsworth (1988) tells us that he saw, while wandering over valleys and hills, a host of golden daffodils at the lakeside fluttering and dancing in the breeze. In the final stanza, Wordsworth explains that, in moments of tranquility, the occurrence of emotive-charged images of this earlier experience of natural beauty took poetic shape.

For oft, when on my couch I lie
In vacant or pensive mood,
They flash upon that inward eye
Which is the bliss of solitude;
And then my heart with pleasure fills,
And dances with the daffodils. (p.205)

We learn from these testimonies that imagery plays a major role in the act of creative imagination. Whether in the problem-solving or reflective mode, images contribute insights to great scientific discoveries or lead to inspired musical and poetic compositions. In rare moments, creative geniuses tap on the cosmic for inspiration and direction, experience images, and find illumination for creative production.

## ART AND IMAGERY

Art depends on the external environment internalized as images, in the first instance, for its materials. These mental images are processed by the creative imagination to produce fresh image combinations eventually expressed in a figural art form that includes drawing, painting, and sculpting.

> Art is involved with the making of actual image forms. But creation of an actual image must be preceded by a mental image. In the visual arts these mental images are visual; in music they are audible. (Preble, 1973, p. 14)

Rosemary Gordon (1972) explains that different people involved in different art forms need various kinds of image combinations. For instance, imagery needed by the dramatist, filmmaker, theater director, and artist is primarily visual, whereas imagery needed by the musician is primarily auditory. Furthermore, the imagery of artists varies from culture to culture. As illustration, Gordon suggests that a Chinese artist may sketch London, which resembles a city in China.

According to Silvano Arieti (1976), artists paint what they perceive. If they paint from memory rather than by looking at what they see, like earlier artists who painted in caves in the absence of their subjects, they resort to imagery. However, artists who rely on imagery first have to perceive their objects before they can evoke them through imagery (see Figure 4.1).

Artists today are less inclined to reproduce the visual world in mirror-like fashion, but rather represent their view of it. This is congruent with Pablo Picasso's observation that nature and art are just two different things and cannot be made the same. It is not the purpose of the artist to imitate nature, but to create life as nature does and to express an inner reality more enduring than the shifting impressions of everyday life (Preble, 1973). Hence, artists depended more on imagery and imagination, rather than on perception and memory, for a fuller and more profound expression of the human spirit.

## THE LANGUAGE OF ART

Brommer and Kohl (1988) and Feldman (1981) have observed art as consisting of visual elements and visual grammar, just as the verbal language consists of an alphabet-vocabulary and grammar-syntax. The function of both these languages have been established through usage. Visual elements, such as line, shape, shading and darkness, color, and texture, constitute one aspect of the language of art. These elements, organized or structured by principles of design to give a totality of meaning to an artwork, constitute the other aspect of the language of art.

Art has a language all its own (J. Khatena, 1997; N. Khatena, 1995). We view that its symbolic form is the *figural motif* that labels image experiences for manipulation by the creative imagination for production of a work of art. *Figural motifs*, symbolic abstracts of the physical universe, make up the alphabet of art. Drawn from natural phenomena, such as waves, mountains, sun, human beings, fish, animals, plant life, and fire, these *motifs* constitute the seven alphabetical units of visual art—the *spiral, circle, semicircle, two semicircles, wavy line, zigzag,* and *straight line*—as illustrated in Figure 6.1 to Figure 6.7.

**Figure 6.1** Right and Left Spiral Motif. Copyright © 1983 by Nelly Khatena. Reprinted by permission.

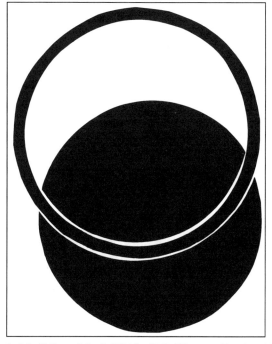

**Figure 6.2** Circle Motif. Copyright © 1983 by Nelly Khatena. Reprinted by permission.

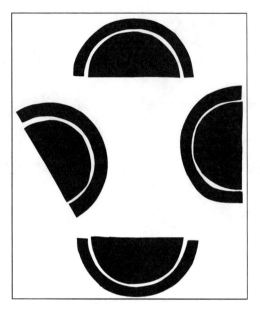

**Figure 6.3**  Semicircle Motif. Copyright © 1983 by Nelly Khatena. Reprinted by permission.

**Figure 6.4**  Two Semicircles Motif. Copyright © 1983 by Nelly Khatena. Reprinted by permission.

**Figure 6.5** Wavy Line Motif. Copyright © 1983 by Nelly Khatena. Reprinted by permission.

**Figure 6.6** Zigzag Motif. Copyright © 1983 by Nelly Khatena. Reprinted by permission.

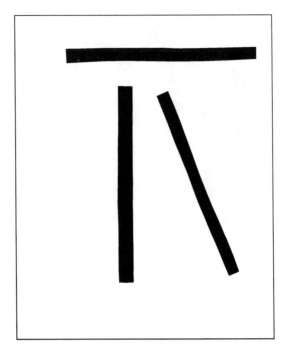

**Figure 6.7** Straight Line Motif. Copyright © 1983 by Nelly Khatena. Reprinted by permission.

Extensions of these are illustrated as a spiral in reverse, combined motif patterns, circle patterns, semicircle patterns, semicircles reversed to make wave patterns, and patterns of straight and zigzag lines (Figure 6.8 to Figure 6.14).

**Figure 6.8** Right and Left Spiral Design. © 1983 by Nelly Khatena. Reprinted by permission.

**Figure 6.9** Combined Motif Patterns. © 1983 by Nelly Khatena. Reprinted by permission.

**Figure 6.10**   Circle Patterns. Copyright © 1983 by Nelly Khatena. Reprinted by permission.

**Figure 6.11**   Semicircle Patterns. © 1983 by Nelly Khatena. Reprinted by permission.

**Figure 6.12** Semicircle Reverse Patterns. Copyright © 1983 by Nelly Khatena. Reprinted by permission.

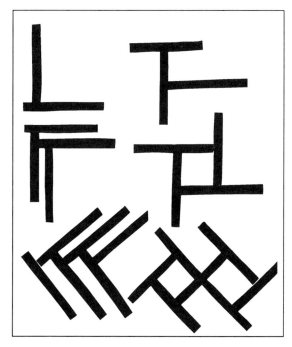

**Figure 6.13** Straight Line Patterns. Copyright © 1983 by Nelly Khatena. Reprinted by permission.

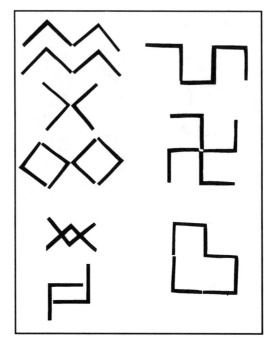

**Figure 6.14**   Zigzag Line Patterns. Copyright © 1983 by Nelly Khatena. Reprinted by permission.

Adolf Best-Maugard (1952) explains that these seven motifs, derived from the ideal spiral that develops in all dimensions and is cosmic in origin, are basic to design in art. Its eternal energy is expressed in vortical motion acting on matter to produce all forms in the universe. Specific instances of these are to be found in:

a) atmospheric phenomena appearing as the vortical movement of air or water that is visible in whirlwinds, whirlpools, gases, waves, or flames of fire;
b) plant life, which can be seen in the structure and growth of vegetables, the arrangement of leaves and branches, and the arrangement of feathers on birds and scales on fish;
c) astronomy, which can be seen in the shapes of nebulae and the orbits of celestial bodies; and
d) microscopic structure, as well as in the motion of electrons and atoms.

This led Best-Maugard (1952) to indicate that "the whirling spiral in nature, as it relates to the plastic arts, provides the fundamentals of design, which when projected on a one-dimensional surface, yields the *seven motifs* common to all primitive art" (Khatena & Khatena, 1990, p. 29).

We may conceptualize the *seven motifs* as originating from various paths taken by a single particle set in motion by some force varying from the straight or zigzag line to the wave or spiral. The motifs, taken together, represent an ideal population of shapes, whose frequent recurrence in nature give rise to the seven motifs (Khatena & Khatena, 1990) identified to serve as the alphabet of visual art.

Just as the English language has a system of 26 letters (A–Z), a language of numbers comprised of nine basic numerals (0–9), and a language of music comprised of eight basic notes (A–G), the language of art has a system of seven figural motifs basic to composition and communication. Of these four language systems, the verbal is culturebound, whereas the numerical, musical, and figural motifs are universal.

These motifs express themselves in many visual forms. We need only to observe stairways, window grills, decorations on the overhangs of buildings, furniture, clothing, jewels, and all kinds of art forms, primitive or contemporary, to see one or more of the seven motifs in action. Motifs found in natural objects are sometimes not only common to one another, but also common to products we make.

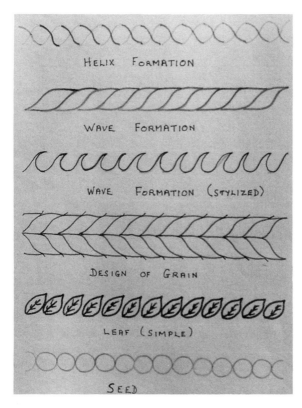

**Figure 6.15**   Wave Motif in Plant Life. © 1983 by Nelly Khatena. Reprinted by permission.

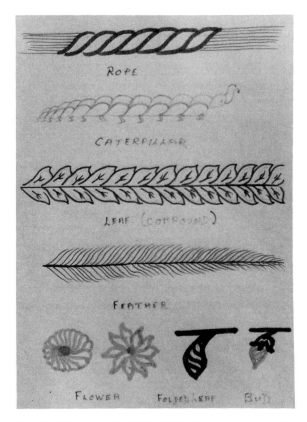

**Figure 6.16** Wave Motif Patterns. © 1983 by Nelly Khatena. Reprinted by permission.

Nelly Khatena (1995; Khatena & Khatena, 1990) perceives the seed as the fertilizing agent of conception. In plant life, for instance, grass seeds or grains of wheat have the configuration of the wave motif, in that when combined in reverse, takes the form of the helix. Taking the wave motif of the seed, she transforms it into a simple or frontal view of a leaf, a compound or folded leaf, a bud and a flower, a feather, a caterpillar, and a rope (Figure 6.15 and Figure 6.16).

**Figure 6.17** Wave Motif Forming Snail. Copyright © 1983 by Nelly Khatena. Reprinted by permission.

She also shows how the wave motif can be formed into a shell and a snail, or a duck (goose) and a bird, or a rabbit (mouse, cat) and a dog (fox, wolf) (Figure 6.17 to Figure 6.19).

WAVE PATTERN

DUCK, GEESE.

BIRD

**Figure 6.18** Wave Motif Forming Birds. Copyright © 1983 by Nelly Khatena. Reprinted by permission.

Furthermore, the wave motif is developed from a leaf to a seal, a turtle, and a dinosaur (Figure 6.20).

A closer look at these simple artistic representations will show that in fact all seven motifs occur: the wave is a semicircle continued in reverse (e.g., leaf, shell); the circle is a combination of two half-circles directly facing each other (e.g., dog eye, flower

**Figure 6.19**  Wave Motif Forming Animals. Copyright © 1983 by Nelly Khatena. Reprinted by permission.

center); several half-circles in continuous reverse flow create the spiral (e.g., caterpillar, rope); and the straight and zigzag lines are used to make the shape of certain body components of animals (e.g., bird beak, tortoise feet).

**Figure 6.20** Wave Motif from Plant to Animal. Copyright © 1983 by Nelly Khatena. Reprinted by permission.

One work of art, entitled *Swanee* (Figure 6.21), by Nelly Khatena, is reproduced here to illustrate the language of art processed by creative imagination. The content of the picture is that of a stylized swan whose feathers are like leaves. The wave motif used illustrates the head and body of the swan, the bird's claws, and its leaflike feathers.

Nelly Khatena's artworks took a mature turn in the development of what has become her signature: the "Egg Series." One in the series is a work entitled *Ginko* (see Figure A, in the color insert in the center of this volume). Ginko is the Chinese name for silver fruit. She takes its basic form and transforms it into a work of art within the form of an egg or oval shape.

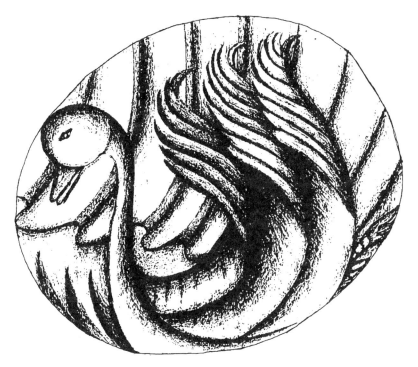

**Figure 6.21**   *Swanee.* Copyright © 1986 by Nelly Khatena. Reprinted by permission.

Nelly Khatena describes the ginko as:

…a tree with fan-shaped leaves, much like the leaf of a maidenhair fern. The leaves are light green, turning darker by mid-summer, and yellow in autumn. The fleshy covering of the seeds of the ginko tree bursts asunder in readiness for its falling and propagation, and at which time it emits an offensive odor.

I first saw the ginko in South Carolina and was most impressed by its beautiful fan-like leaf. Observing it again on the campus of Mississippi State University, I noted more carefully the structure of the tree, the shape of its leaves, flowers, fruit, and color. I was by now convinced that I had the beginnings of a lovely work of art. The idea of a fan-shaped work within an egg became firmly established in my mind.

The following principles of design and content guided her creative imagination as she began to give life to the work:

| Design Principles | Artistic Fan | Ginko Tree |
|---|---|---|
| Style | Stylized | Biomorphic or organic |
| Rhythm | 3 different fan sizes | Different sizes and positions woven into a fan to make for interesting rhythm |
| | Repetition of fan wood skeleton | |
| | Asymmetrical repetition of ginko leaves | |
| | Branches straight, different sizes | Branches curved, different sizes |
| Color | Branches black | Branches black |
| | Body green | Leaves complimentary |
| | Black, white, green, yellow | to color of fan body (green) |
| Balance | Color and branches | Color, branches and leaves |
| | Segments of fan | |
| Movement | Intertwining of branches | Direction of curved trunk, branches, leaves, flowers, and fruit |
| Unity in variety | Little fan at bottom, mid-fan, whole fan | Ginko leaves |
| Tone | Overall even | Overall even |

Like a musical composition, the *Ginko* is harmonious and aesthetic within the egg. It contains motifs of the straight line (branches–fan skeleton), the semicircle (ginko leaves–fan), the semicircle in reverse or wave (bimorfic structure of plant and artwork), and the circle (silver fruit). The creative imaginative processes of synthesis and analogy were used to combine the elements together to effect a transformation showing an analogous relationship between the *Ginko* and fan, and illustrating nature's extension of a human endeavor.

## CONCLUSION

In this chapter, two language systems were discussed. Imagery has been described as the language of discovery. Its sensory roots acquire information from the external environment and, converted to images, they become the source of discovery and invention. According to many testimonies of creative geniuses, creative imagination acts upon them to produce an original work. In addition, art has its own language, whose alphabet lies in generic figural motifs derived from examples of nature. When acted upon by creative imagination, these motifs emerge as original and beautiful works of art. Chapter 7 explores design as order and composition in art.

# 7

## Art Composition as Design

### OVERVIEW

The chapter begins by describing the concepts of order and disorder as it relates to nature, the environment, and the universe, from which spring forth the fundamentals of design. Elizabethan World Order, being one instance of this, prepares the way for a more universal order-disorder theory described as general systems. The chapter continues with a discussion of design principles in art that provides the grammar and syntax for visual elements, seen as seven generic motifs derived from natural phenomena. In addition, several design principles are illustrated, which provide the bases for the structuring and composing of visual art.

### INTRODUCTION

Any discussion of design must begin with the concept of order, as emerging from the arrangement of hitherto unrelated elements into a coherent interrelated structure. It is intentional planning that gives meaning and harmony to what is around us. Design makes our environment comprehensible. To understand design, we need only to open ourselves to our natural surroundings and allow nature to be our teacher. For by so doing, we will see unlimited varieties of forms with species-specific functions, in whose interrelationship exists the fundamentals of design.

We have learned that what goes on in nature is not haphazard, but highly ordered. What once was perceived as random occurrences has been discovered as the outcome of an intelligence, operating according to certain universal laws. These laws of nature design and unify the existence and function of the universe. They constitute the principles of design that guide all forms of human activity toward productive ends.

## ELIZABETHAN WORLD ORDER

E. M. W. Tillyard (1956), an authority on Shakespeare's history plays, suggested that to gain a proper understanding of plays such as *Richard II* and *Henry IV*, it would be best if we knew how Elizabethans regarded the world at that time. So that we could do this, Tillyard sketched the system of thought that governed Elizabethan belief and behavior in a book entitled *Elizabethan World Picture* (1958).

According to this system, macro order prevailing in heaven is projected in microcosm on earth, such that the king on earth is like God in heaven, or, in terms of heavenly bodies, the king resembles the sun. If disorder occurred in the heavens, it would bring about earthly disorder. Everything was connected in a *chain-of-being*, from the highest archangels through Man to the lowest forms of life.

*Degree*, or hierarchical order, was a key concept related to what Tillyard (1958) called the vertical dimension of the world picture. A horizontal organization of the world picture consisted of an immense network of *corresponding planes*, its interrelationships ordered according to degrees of dignity. From highest to lowest, corresponding planes of influence began with the divine and angelic, the universe or macrocosm, the commonwealth or body politic, Man or microcosm, going down the scale to the lower orders of creation. From the thought of the early Greek philosophers was derived the notion that creation was an act of music, with each sphere of influence emitting a musical sound that when combined made the *harmony of the spheres*. Furthermore, the created universe itself was in a state of perpetual dance, implying *degree in motion*.

In Elizabethen times, principles of design in nature included a vertical hierarchical ordering of the universe and nature on the one hand, and a horizontal ordering of elemental groupings, themselves hierarchically organized within each plane, on the other. Within complex networks of interrelationships between horizontal and vertical ordering were yet other important design principles. The creative and unifying design factor lay in the concept of music, harmony, and motion. For the Elizabethans, this was their conception of the universe, a general system that evolved from their religion, philosophy, politics, and general way of life.

## GENERAL SYSTEMS

In recent times, several scholars, such as Stuart Dodd, Derald Langham, George Land, and John Gowan, drawing from advances in scientific and mathematical thought, have attempted to find general principles to explain existence and human behavior. They categorized their findings as *general systems*, which are based on generic principles aimed at discovering ever-increasing levels of order. According to George Land (1973), a general system is a means by which fundamental laws of nature discovered can be applied in theory and practice to everything. Land describes his general system as *The Unifying Principle of Transformation*. It gives meaning to his concept of *Grow or Die*, which is the title of his book.

### Grow or Die

According to Land (1973), a general system consists of the polar opposite concepts of great disorder and great order. Connections between them are by *dominance* and *absorption* to achieve control. In the first stage, disorder gives way to order so that an identity or order pattern emerges, which he calls the *accretive stage*.

This first stage prepares the way for the second stage, whereby the pattern achieved in the *accretive stage* is copied, with a few changes. Land calls this the *replicative stage*. Relationships in this stage are one of influence and being influenced.

Since there is a pattern to follow, growth towards the third stage is rapid. The environment is used up and the pattern is forced to accommodate differences if growth is to continue. Sensitive and responsive to the environment, the relationships shift to mutual sharing, just because it works best. Land (1973) calls this the *mutualistic stage*.

Once differences in the environment have been absorbed and shared, they become new sameness, and a new identity is formed. A new disorder occurs to become the basis for the establishment of a new order at a higher level. Land (1973) calls the end result of this process the *transformative stage*.

In summary, Land (1973) calls the first three stages *accretive*, *replicative*, and *mutualistic*, respectively. The fourth stage he calls *transformative*, a transitory stage from a lower to a higher level of growth, where order gives way to disorder so that a reordering can emerge at a higher level.

In terms of the physiobiochemical processes of evolution, this process is illustrated by *mutation* and *hybridization*. Land (1982) explains that in *mutation* occurs random rearrangement, substitution, addition, or deletion of small portions of DNA, which prepares the way for *hybridization*, or the emergence of new forms and functions. In this way, Land offers a viable view of design, its principles rooted in the laws of nature.

## DESIGN IN ART

To continue what we have said about the language of art, design principles serve as the grammar and syntax of visual elements, which we have identified and shall develop further as the seven generic motifs. At this point, let us distinguish between the rules of grammar and syntax that govern verbal language from their visual counterparts, which does not operate as strictly. However, the language of art needs consistent application of organization to maximize the effectiveness of an artwork, no matter what purpose or meaning is intended.

According to Duan Preble (1973), the principles of design in art take life from the laws of nature, for human design is but an extension of nature's design. What art and nature design share in common is growth from within by an inner necessity to achieve order and its refined correlate, harmony. Just as design in nature concerns itself with the interrelationship of a form and its function, design in art concerns itself with the arrangement of a work's elements in harmonious unifying relationship. As design in nature makes our environment comprehensible, design in art gives meaning to a work of art.

In the visual arts, the structuring or ordering of elements into a whole involves both designing and/or composing. This process is often spontaneous or intuitive. Whereas *designing* a work of art is more directly related to determining its architecture, using the guidelines of certain principles, *composing* goes beyond the aspect of planning to include creative use of the imagination to generate the new.

Adolf Best-Maugard (1952) suggested that general principles of design drawn from natural phenomena (for example, waves, mountains, sun, human beings, fish, animals, plant life, and fire) are basic to design in art. They are manifested in seven fundamental motifs—the spiral, circle, semicircle, two semicircles, wavy line, zigzag, and straight line—on which all primitive art is based. We have already indicated that a distinction needs to be made between the language of art, whose symbols lie in these motifs, and the *process* that shapes or designs it into a unified work. The operation of process, according to Duan Preble and Sarah Preble (1978), is governed by the principles of design, which include scale, proportion, variety within unity, repetition and rhythm, balance, directional forces, emphasis and subordination, and contrast.

## Scale

*Scale* in a work of art is a principle of design that refers to its size relative to the observer. For instance, an artist may make an impact by painting things larger than the human scale. Furthermore, a small work may be made to look monumentally large, or a large work, appearing intricate or delicate, may be sensed as smaller than its actual size. Everything perceived is relative. An example of this can be seen in the relative height of two people—the tallness of a man is exaggerated when he is standing next to a short woman. Furthermore, scale may also be observed in the relative size of objects in a work of art. For instance, *Fanfare* (Figure 7.1), by Nelly Khatena, shows a large fan serving as a backdrop for the creation of smaller fans, which take the forms of a hat, a skirt, a blouse, a pagoda, and an umbrella.

**Figure 7.1**  *Fanfare.* Copyright © 1988 by Nelly Khatena. Reprinted by permission.

## Proportion

*Proportion* is the size relationship of parts to a whole and to one another. An instance of this can be seen in *Ginko* (see Figure A, in the color insert in the center of this volume), by Nelly Khatena, described in Chapter 6. Notice the three different-sized fans woven proportionately into one large fan, all of which take life from the fan-shaped leaf of the ginko.

## Variety within Unity

*Variety within unity* relates to the diversity of elements within an artwork that become unified and presented as a whole. Interest is provided by variety; but for it to have coherence, the constituent elements must be interrelated and unified. In this way, variety within unity achieves a balanced interest.

*Ginko* (Figure A) illustrates this well in the diversity of gingko-fan shapes, from the small fans at the bottom, to the medium-sized fans in the middle, to the large fan as a whole. These various ginko-fan shapes are integrated to achieve unity. Another aspect of variety within unity relates to the many different straight and curved branches of different sizes, essential to the overall form.

*Fanfare* (Figure 7.1) also illustrates this in the way the artist uses the fan as the basic form for the creation of a picture that so finely integrates a variety of objects, such as people with fan headdresses, umbrellas, fan decorations on kimonos, fan-topped pagodas, and fan-shaped ginko leaves, which take life from the basic fan shape.

## Repetition and Rhythm

*Repetition and rhythm* indicates a reoccurrence of elements in a work of art that contribute to its continuity, flow, and dramatic emphasis. In repetition, visual elements are produced to appear exactly similar or are produced in a variety of ways to establish the rhythm of the piece, just as meter in poetry and time signature in music establish rhythmic measures. The *Ginko* (Figure A) is a good illustration of repetition and rhythm, into which is woven three different-sized and positioned fans into a unified fan. Furthermore, repetition of the wooden skeleton, asymmetrical repetition of the ginko leaves, and repetition of different-sized straight and curved branches should be noted as contributing to the visual rhythm of the piece.

## Balance

*Balance* relates to tension of opposing forces organized to achieve a state of rest. A familiar case is that of scales to measure weight, whereby, suspended on a vertical axis, the weight of an actual object is compared to a standard weight. When the two weights are equal the components of the scale are balanced, or *symmetrical*; if one weight is greater than the other, the components of the scale become *asymmetrical*, or leaning to one side or the other.

In a work of art, when elements organized along an actual or implied central axis are similar or identical, the work is said to have symmetrical balance, or *bilateral symmetry*. This form of symmetry is the simplest and most static form of balance. When elements radiate from or converge on an actual or implied central point, they are said to have *radial balance*. This kind of balance is analogical to that of a wheel with spokes radiating from its hub to its circumference.

Balance may also be attained through the absence of symmetry. *Asymmetrical* balance appeals to many more artists because of its more subtle, dynamic, and interesting effects. By it, elements of varying visual weights are pulled together to achieve a state of equilibrium.

Balance is also found in the way color is used. In particular, balance is achieved by the selection of colors that harmoniously interrelate. For instance, red and black are two primary colors that command attention. Too much of either color draws the attention of the observer away from the rest of the composition. Consequently, it is essential for the artist to exercise care in the way red or black is used.

Balance of color can be created through the use of contrast. This may be achieved by color hue, by the use of bright-dull color for saturation, and by the use

**Figure 7.2** *Ice Crystals.* Copyright © 1989 by Nelly Khatena. Reprinted by permission.

of warm-cool color to indicate temperature. If black were to be used as a background in a work, by contrast, colors in the foreground would appear iridescent.

*Radial balance* is illustrated in *Gingko* (Figure A). Note how the bottom of the fan serves as the center of the fan's wooden structure, which radiates in reverse to the top.

Another instance of balance at work can be found in Nelly Khatena's work entitled *Ice Crystals* (Figure 7.2). This is a geometrical composition showing shapes bursting out like a flower in the sun. In it are combined features of balance that are both radial and asymmetrical.

*The Balance of Power* (Figure 7.3), by Nelly Khatena, is yet another composition that illustrates balance. The composition within the egg shape overflows into a rectangular space, giving greater and more subtle dimension to the artwork. The content is evocative of balance, both literally and metaphorically. A pair of scales provides an instance of bilateral balance, while the three houses of government (executive, legislative, and judicial) and their functions are intricately woven into an asymmetrical balance of telling beauty. Other elements include the White House, an eagle, the American flag with its stars and stripes, the Jefferson Memorial, and Pennsylvania Avenue. The large star on the right provides asymmetrical balance to the Washington Monument, hidden behind the egg shape. Furthermore, the vertical pillars in the foreground, the slender vertical lines of the pediment, and the stripes of the flag at the base of the work are asymmetrically balanced against the radial struc-

**Figure 7.3** *The Balance of Power.* © 1987 by Nelly Khatena. Reprinted by permission.

ture of the courthouse in the background and the sun's rays at the top right-hand corner of the work.

### Directional Forces

*Directional forces* operating in a work of art relate to linear lines, seen or implied, which provide direction and basic structure to the work. The wooden structure of *Ginko* (Figure A) illustrates well the function of directional forces. An implied line may suggest imagined connection between similar or adjacent forms and can be seen in the way the wooden structure and branches of the fan-shaped ginko intertwine. The unseen axis is another instance of an implied line, which gives dominant direction to a single form or symmetrical design.

Lines may be vertical, horizontal, or diagonal. Whereas vertical and horizontal lines convey the impression or feeling of inaction or rest, diagonal lines create tension, disrupting our sense of gravity to give the impression of motion. This implied movement is the source of the content and mood of a design. Lines that are vertical and horizontal in a design interacting with diagonals generate a strong center of interest visually, such as those in *The Balance of Power* (Figure 7.3). When lines of visual force or energy are not visible but implied, they give the impression of connecting in various ways all kinds of single elements or groups of elements in the design. Perceptions of these are dependent on the individual viewer and are also called subjective lines.

The operation of directional forces is clearly illustrated in another work, entitled *The Big Apple* (Figure B, in the color insert in the center of this volume), by Nelly Khatena. The focal point of this work is the top of the Empire State Building, located to the left of its center. The sun's rays and the skyscrapers, the cables of the Brooklyn Bridge, and the funnels of the riverboat all converge toward the Empire State Building, which in turn points to a red apple, symbolic of New York. Together, the intersecting lines of the cables of the Brooklyn Bridge and the sides of the riverboat create tension, giving the impression of movement. Furthermore, the directional border of black-top taxicabs creates the illusion of continuous movement, symbolizing New York as "the city that never sleeps."

## Emphasis and Subordination

*Emphasis and subordination* refers to the way a member of a group of elements is made to stand out above the rest. For example, the three major pillars in the foreground of *The Balance of Power* (Figure 7.3) emphasizes the three houses of government, subordinating the horizontal stripes of the flag and structure of the pediment.

## Contrast

*Contrast* can be used in a work of art to emphasize the interaction of contradictory elements. It is a way of expressing duality by the juxtaposition of opposites. The thick and thin of a brush stroke, for instance, provides *line contrast*.

Contrast can also be produced with shapes that may be regular geometric and irregular organic shapes. Light and dark areas of a surface offer value contrasts. Other ways to achieve contrasts are by color, hue, saturation (bright-dull color), or temperature (warm-cool color), and between solid mass and empty space.

Good examples of contrast can be found in Nelly Khatena's artworks. For instance, *Ginko* (Figure A) contains effective contrast between the regular geometric and irregular organic shapes in the rigid structure of the fan's skeleton and the bimorphic forms of its leaves and branches. In *The Balance of Power* (Figure 7.3), the broad pillars offer a contrast with the narrow stripes of the flag and pediment structure. Furthermore, the big pointer star on the right side of the work contrasts well with the small stars of the flag and the necklace of stars connected to the pans of the scales.

To recapitulate, it should be noted that although each of the design principles was dealt with in turn, their separation was done for the purpose of discussion. The principles of design found illustration in several of Nelly Khatena's artworks. However, each work must be viewed beyond the design principles for its total effect on the observer. As a whole, each artwork illustrates the artists' observation and view of the world, as well as her creative imagination that produced a thing of great beauty for the appreciation and pleasure of others.

## CONCLUSION

This chapter discusses the concepts of order and disorder taking life from nature with the observation that order in nature is not random, but ever evolving. Principles of design in art were described as the grammar and syntax of visual elements, manifested in seven generic motifs derived from natural phenomena whose function oscillated between structuring and composing. Design principles were discussed and appropriately illustrated in artworks by Nelly Khatena. Chapter 8 deals with creative imagination as a process and a teachable skill.

# 8

# Creative Thinking and Problem Solving Applied to Art

## OVERVIEW

This chapter deals with creative imagination as a process and a teachable skill. These include intellectual abilities, divergent thinking, and several creative problem-solving approaches. A discussion on the application of the principles of these methods to art composition, with relevant illustration by Nelly Khatena, follows.

## INTRODUCTION

According to Albert Einstein, imagination is more important than knowledge, for imagination breathes life into knowledge, giving it shape and form. Imagination, as has been discussed, draws its life-giving energy from the cosmos for vision, action, and expression of high creativity. Ordinary levels of creativity occur when imagination relies on mental-emotive operations to process information, upon which most of us depend for our creative acts.

It is commonly accepted that the potential to be creative is possessed by everyone. This potential is manifested through the use of inherited mental operations, drawing dynamism from its emotional base as it interacts with the environment. By observing how individuals engaged in the creative act process information, we have identified several approaches used by them to produce unique creative outcomes.

# INTELLECTUAL ABILITIES CREATIVELY
# PROCESS INFORMATION

These approaches use *intellectual abilities* organized in a number of ways for the emergence of creativity, the most commonly known of which are divergent thinking, creative problem solving, synthesis-destructuring-restructuring, and metaphor-analogy. This chapter will deal with divergent thinking and creative problem solving, while Chapter 9 will deal with synthesis-destructuring-restructuring and metaphor analogy. No matter how our intellect is organized, it needs *information* to manipulate and fashion for creative ends. The information may take figural, verbal (symbolic-semantic), and behavioral forms. These are organized in different ways by the approaches indicated for creative expression. Just as the writer, for instance, communicates the consequences of processing information creatively in poetic or dramatic form, the visual artist communicates the product of imagination in drawing, painting, or sculpting.

## Divergent Thinking

Any discussion of *divergent thinking* calls to mind the "Structure of Intellect," a three-dimensional model of intellectual activity proposed by J. P. Guilford (1977). One dimension, which is hereditary based, is called *mental operations. Contents*, the second dimension, is dependent on information derived from the environment. Mental operations that act upon informational content to create outcomes is what Guilford calls *products*. This three-way relationship is interactive and represents intellectual abilities (see Figure 8.1).

Divergent thinking is one of five mental operations (see shaded part of Figure 8.1); the others are cognition, memory, convergent thinking, and evaluation. Of the five, divergent thinking is directly associated with creative imagination. It acts on various kinds of information categorized as figural, symbolic, semantic, and behavioral contents. The artist uses, in the main, information of a figural nature to fashion creative works. We have already seen that such information is symbolized as motifs to become the language of art. This means that the artist can create art that directly represents the environment. The artist may choose not to engage in representing nature, but to compose an imaginative and artistic rendition of it. In doing so, the artist becomes involved in transforming the real world into visionary reality.

In representing the real world the artist largely uses *convergent thinking* processes, for to imitate nature is not only to recognize it, but to reproduce, as nearly as possible, its elements and events. This is not the case with divergent thinking, as the artist, in using this, refashions nature to present existing forms in new and fantastic ways. While in the end both approaches may result in works of art, the former approximates the reproductive while the latter is productive. Hence, the artist who relies on divergent thinking to produce art becomes a creator.

A number of mental abilities associated with divergent thinking are fluency, flexibility, elaboration, and originality. An artist involved in creating a work may exhibit the use of one or more of these abilities. According to J. P. Guilford (1968), the first

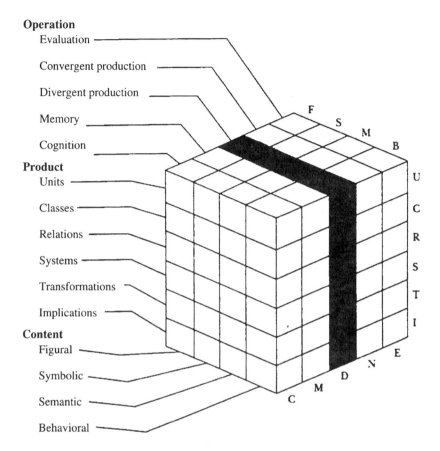

**Figure 8.1** The "Structure of Intellect" Model. Reprinted by permission from Guilford, 1967, p. 63.

three of these abilities (that is, fluency, flexibility, and elaboration) in the figural dimension is important in art, for the artist communicates meaning in nonverbal or figural ways. Originality, involving artistic production of the new, incorporates fluency, flexibility, and elaboration.

Guilford (1968) breaks down *fluency* in the figural information area into *ideational fluency*, or the ability to generate many ideas; *analogy fluency*, or the ability to produce many analogues; and *expressional fluency*, or the ability to rapidly organize figural information as systems.

*Flexibility* relates to two kinds of abilities that involve shifts in thinking from one category or class of information to another. *Spontaneous flexibility* indicates automatic shifts in thinking, whereas *adaptive flexibility* points to shifts in thinking due to the need for different solutions to a single problem.

According to J. P. Guilford (1968), *elaboration* is very important to art. In the early stages of a creative production, details may be added once a general schema or plan develops to become a distinct psychological system.

To illustrate the use of these elements of divergent thinking, let us take Nelly Khatena's work entitled *Fanfare* (Figure 7.1). The artwork is a superb example of the use of divergent thinking, its basic figural content being the ginko motif.

Central to the design is the egg shape, which represents the body of a fan, its lines extending to the bottom right-hand corner in the form of a fan handle to complete its total structure. It is interesting to note how the lines of the handle, in projecting upward, serve as the skeletal structure of three distinct fan components that together make up the fan-shaped body of the egg (elaboration).

In the foreground and vicinity of the fan handle are three ginko leaves, placed as if to say that everything else in the picture is made by human design. Only the veins of each leaf, the lines dividing segments of the fan, branches of the ginko decoration on the umbrella and kimono of the Japanese girl, and the scarf, skirt waistline, and sandals of the woman to the right are in the main curved; other ginko-like forms (analogy fluency) in the shape of umbrellas, pagodas, hats, and plaited hair, upon whose ends are suspended fans, have straight skeletal structure (spontaneous flexibility). These many analogical elements of the ginko are combined in a figural system to produce an aesthetic piece of art (expressional fluency). The many decorative features within each of the analogical objects of the ginko, like the floral pattern on the dress of the central Japanese woman or the details on the umbrella, enhances the picture (elaboration). Notice too the outflow from the egg-shaped component into the rectangle, which creates a harmonious picture, its total aesthetic effect beautiful, delightful, and unique (originality).

In creating this work of art, the artist had also to use *cognition*: Her knowledge of the constituent environmental elements (for example, ginko, fan, umbrella, Japanese woman, pagoda) were at first cognitively processed. Their combining to shape a single artistic expression involved the use of *convergent thinking*. In addition, from the many possible elements the artist could have drawn, she selected those of the picture. This selection called for the use of *evaluation*. The many ways the elements could have been combined and the emergent combination required a fine interplay between convergent and divergent thinking processes. Throughout this art composition, evaluation maintained a delicate balance between stretching the imagination through stages of the creative process and deferring judgment to effect too early a closure.

According to Sidney J. Parnes and Angelo Biondi (1975), if judgment is not to overwhelm the imagination in decision making, a *deferjudice* stance must be maintained to allow for the comfortable oscillation between *nojudice* and *prejudice*, *looseness*, and *tightness*, with full awareness that nothing is final. All these processes at work during art composition are not necessarily consciously exercised, though an artist may be made aware of the mental activity that goes on.

## Creative Problem Solving

The "Structure of Intellect" model provides the roots for a generic problem-solving model (Guilford, 1977). It is a system that organizes the five mental operations of the intellect to creatively solve problems. The environment provides informational input through the senses of the body and uses essentially all previously acquired information, either in its original or processed form, in memory storage.

We have already shown how divergent thinking is used by an artist to create a work of art, as illustrated in Figure 7.1. The production of this work is also related to the processes of Guilford's (1977) generic creative problem-solving model, whereby the problem encountered by the artist was to produce a composition reflecting Man's extension of nature in human terms. Specifically, the artist chose the ginko as a basic natural form and showed its extension in things we make, like the fan, umbrella, pagoda, hat, and skirt, in a Japanese context. Input from the environment, particularly relating to Japanese experiences and artistic feelings about them "recollected in tranquility," was processed by the "Structure of Intellect" mechanisms and the creative imagination with the purpose of finding a solution or resolution to the problem. The outcome was a beautiful work of art, its harmony and integrity directly related to the use of sound principles of design.

Many approaches of creative problem solving, based on *sequential steps*, have been proposed. Among the leaders of the earlier sequential steps model are John Dewey (1910), Joseph Rossman (1931), James Vargiu (1977), and Graham Wallas (1926) (Table 8.1).

### Table 8.1
### Creative Problem Solving Sequential-Step Approaches

| John Dewey | Joseph Rossman | James Vargiu | Graham Wallas |
| --- | --- | --- | --- |
| Difficulty felt | Need or difficulty observed | | |
| Difficulty located and defined | Problem formulated Available information surveyed | | |
| | | Preparation or information collected | Preparation Frustration |
| Possible solution suggestions | Solutions formulated | Illumination or emergent solutions | Solutions Avalanche effect |
| Consequences considered | Solutions examined critically | Verification or testing Elaborating solutions | Elaboration |
| Solution accepted | New ideas formulated New ideas tested and accepted | | |

Reprinted by permission from Khatena, 1982, p. 278.

## John Dewey

According to John Dewey (1910), problem solving involves: 1) sensing a difficulty; 2) locating and defining the difficulty; 3) suggesting possible solutions; 4) considering consequences; and 5) accepting a solution. Those who followed Dewey either made minor modification to or elaborated on his five problem-solving steps.

## Jospeh Rossman

Jospeh Rossman (1931) derived steps for his model from a study of 700 inventors. These steps consisted of: 1) need or difficulty observed; 2) problem formulated; 3) available information surveyed; 4) solution formulated; and 5) solution evaluated. It should be noted that Rossman added to John Dewey's steps the surveying of available information and formulation of new ideas.

## Graham Wallas

Four creative problem-solving steps comprise the Wallas (1926) model, namely: 1) *preparation*, or information gathering; 2) *incubation*, or mind activity relating to the unconscious processes; 3) *illumination*, or emergent solutions; and 4) *verification*, or acceptance of solutions. Although Wallas does not begin with a step similar to Dewey's (1910) "sensing a difficulty," the step must be implied, as it is what starts the whole problem-solving sequence.

## James Vargiu

Fifty years later, James Vargiu (1977) proposed almost a similar creative problem-solving model to Wallas's, to which were added *confusion* and *frustration* as the steps following preparation, energizing the problem solver to move forward, and *elaboration* was added in place of verification, with the latter implied in the total creative problem-solving process.

Vargiu (1977), theorizing on the subject of incubation-illumination, suggests that the function of imagination may be thought of in terms of the activity of creative energy fields that are both mental and emotive. Drawing on analogies from the world of physics, he tentatively defines the creative process as:

> a large number of simple mental elements within the boundary of a creative energy field which have such properties that (1) each mental element will respond to the influence of the creative field, and (2) all mental elements can interact with one another. (p. 23)

To illustrate this, Vargiu describes the well-known behavior of a thin layer of iron filings in the presence of a magnet:

> At first, the field is too weak to set the iron particles in motion. They are held in position by friction. As the intensity of the magnetic field increases, some of the iron particles overcome friction and begin to move, interacting with the nearby granules in a way that increases the overall magnetization. This in turn sets other particles in motion,

accelerating the process and starting an avalanche effect or chain reaction which causes the pattern to suddenly form itself, independently of any further approach of the
magnet. (p. 13)

According to Vargiu (1977), mental events in problem solving pass through the
stages of preparation, confusion, frustration, incubation, illumination, and elaboration.
The insightful moment or illumination he analogically describes as avalanche effect.

Thus the illumination comes to our consciousness as something new, something unex-
pected. It is produced by the creative field of which we are not aware, and when it
occurs it is beyond our conscious control. So it generates in us the unique and para-
doxical impression of an unknown source that leads to deeper knowing, of a blinding
flash that leads to clearer vision, of a loss of control that leads to greater order. (p. 24)

Prior to illumination is the incubation stage, which Vargiu (1977) suggests is not
a statistically random ordering of mental elements. Instead, it is the dynamism
involved by the creative energy field that, in the initial part of the creative process,
passes through the stages of preparation, confusion, and frustration that lay the
groundwork for incubation, which leads to illumination:

The initial part of the creative process—preparatory activity to confusion and frustration—can thus be seen as having a three-fold purpose: supplying material on which the
creative field can play; overcoming friction by setting this material into motion, thereby making it more responsive to the influence of the creative field; and providing conceptual seeds through which the creative insight relates to the problem. It is common
knowledge among creative people that the intensity of the preparatory stage often
determines how closely the insight will fit the problem. The stages of confusion and
frustration have only a subsidiary function, but are psychological means we may need
to justify saying what amounts to the hell with it, and turning our attention elsewhere.
We then move on to the incubation stage, the crucial and delicate period during which
the often very weak creative field can act on the mental elements without the distur-
bance of our conscious manipulation, and therefore in the cumulative, coherent fashion that leads to illumination. (p. 27)

Vargiu (1977) expands this model to include the emotional field that runs intact
with the mental elements, tending to organize these mental elements into configura-
tions that correspond to their own energy patterns. It is this interaction between the
mental elements and the emotional field that constitutes the very essence of creative
imagination, so that images are formed in the mind and energized by feelings.

All the above suggests that the function of creative imagination involves intellectual abilities as well as energy fields, which operate in various ways to lead to incubation, creative imagery, and illumination in the creative process. Drawing from the
Guilfordian conception of intellectual abilities and Wallas's and Vargiu's ideas on
creativity and problem-solving processes, we may perceive abilities energized by
mental and emotive magnetic fields of forces as central to creative functioning.

Activity set in motion by creative imagination causes these forces to act and interact with each other, and with intellectual abilities. This activity may be deliberate or ongoing, without our full awareness. However, if a problem is presented for processing this activity, incubation is induced and often produces imagery that leads to illumination and problem solution. This is illustrated in Figure 8.2.

The steps of these models form the basic principles of the many available creative problem-solving models. Chief among them, as they have special relevance to artists, are the Osborn–Parnes Creative Problem Solving Model (Osborn, 1962, 1963; Parnes, 1967) and Synectics (Gordon, 1966), with the first being dealt with in this chapter and the second in chapter 9.

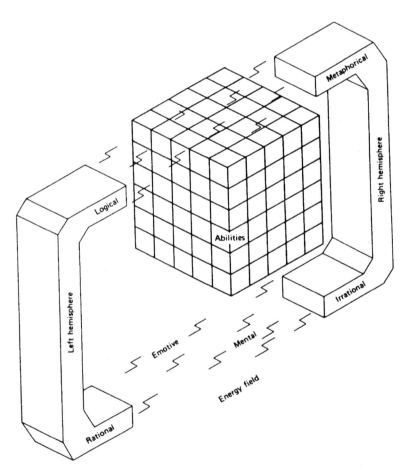

**Figure 8.2** Intellectual Abilities Activated by Energy Fields. Reprinted by permission from Khatena, 1979, p. 6.

## Osborn–Parnes Creative Problem Solving Model

In l963, Alex F. Osborn gave us *Applied Imagination*, in which he discusses principles of creative problem solving not only applicable to an individual, but also to a group. Osborn explains in the preface that creative imagination is possessed to some degree by all people, although many do not know how to use it properly. His formal and systematic aims at teaching people how to utilize the creative imagination more fully. The method advocates that creativity is more than mere imagination that inseparably couples both intent and effort, which can maximize creative processing and its manifestation.

The Osborn–Parnes Creative Problem Solving Method, very widely used over the years, especially with adults, is closely associated with the terms "group-think" and "brainstorming." The method has four ground rules said to lead to effective creative problem solving. Accordingly, 1) criticism is ruled out; 2) freewheeling is encouraged because wild or impractical ideas may spark off other ideas, leading to a breakthrough idea toward a practical solution; 3) quantity of ideas is desired on the assumption that quality, or better, ideas may be produced; and 4) combination and improvement of ideas are facilitated by "hitchhiking" on others' ideas, asking idea-spurring questions, using free association, using analogies, forcing-fit relations (such as putting a square peg in a round hole), using various sense modalities, and so forth.

Keys to Alex F. Osborn's technique of creative problem solving are: 1) deferment of judgment, or the alternation between creative and evaluative thinking, analogically described as green and red traffic light activity; and 2) quantity breeds quality, or the generation of many ideas to provide for the emergence of many more good ideas. Osborn was led to propose a three-step creative problem-solving method (fact-finding, idea-finding, and solution-finding) that incorporates these principles (Osborn, 1962).

> **Fact-finding.** This step consists of two parts: a) problem definition, or picking out and pointing to the problem; and b) preparation, or gathering and analyzing pertinent data.
> **Idea-finding.** Two components of this step involve: a) idea production, or the thinking of tentative ideas as possible leads; and b) idea development, or selecting from resultant ideas, adding others, and reprocessing by means of modification, combination, rearrangement, substitution, and so on.
> **Solution-finding.** This step is comprised of two components: a) evaluation or verification of tentative solutions; and b) decision and implementation of the final solution.

According to Sidney J. Parnes (1967), a problem seems unclear and is a fuzzy mess at first to the experiencer. Hence, to define a real problem encountered is difficult without careful exploration to uncover the facts relating to the problem. This is Osborn's (1962) fact-finding step. If sufficient clarity results from the uncovering of related facts, the real problem is likely to be identified. Osborn has called this the problem-finding step. Idea-finding, or individual or group brainstorming, follows. As a consequence, solution-finding occurs, and the generation of alternative solutions follows. Once several solutions are identified, they are evaluated according to several relevant criteria (for example, cost, implementation time, usefulness, and social acceptability). This is followed by acceptance finding to determine the most appropriate solutions for the adoption of a successful action plan.

The Osborn–Parnes Creative Problem Solving Model experienced a shift in the use of imagination and judgment (Parnes, Noller, & Biondi, 1977) since it was first formulated. This meant that both imagination and judgment can occur in every one of the four creative problem solving steps. That is, unleashing the imagination is to be gradual while judicial abilities are concurrently strengthened. Stretching the imagination can occur in all creative problem solving stages, rather than in the idea-generation stage alone. In this way, the problem-definition stage allows for more effort in the acquisition of a multiplicity of viewpoints to the problem. The trick, according to Parnes and Biondi (1975), was to maintain a delicate balance between imagination and judgment when judgment no longer overwhelmed the imagination in decision making, for

> if we maintain the *deferjudice* stance, then we may oscillate comfortably between *nojudice* and *prejudice*; between *openness* and *closedness*; between *looseness* and *tightness*—fully aware that nothing is final. (original emphasis, p. 157)

Sidney J. Parnes's *The Magic of Your Mind* (1981) extends these concepts of creative problem solving to include intuitive imagery and spontaneous imagery. Both imagery processes occur in incubation and autonomous imaging.

In *Visionizing*, Parnes (1988) recommends explicit use of imagery in the context of the earlier problem-solving approach. According to him, spontaneous imagery facilitates *visionizing*, or the activity involved in making a dream come true, for solving a problem of current importance or future relevance.

## PRINCIPLES APPLIED IN NELLY KHATENA'S ART

All these principles are well illustrated in *Fanfare* (Figure 7.1), *Swanee* (Figure 6.29), *Ginko* (Figure A, in the color insert in the center of this volume), *Ice Crystals* (Figure 7.2), *The Balance of Power* (Figure 7.3), and *The Big Apple* (Figure B, in the color insert). In composing these artworks, Nelly Khatena went through the processes of creative problem solving. In terms of the Osborn–Parnes model, for instance, the three stages of fact-finding, idea-finding, and solution-finding were observed, if not deliberately, then intuitively. We may also discuss the creation of her works in terms of Graham Wallas's (1926) paradigm of preparation, incubation, illumination, and verification.

The Osborn–Parnes model's three stages of creative problem solving can be seen in action in Nelly Khatena's artworks. Prior to an art composition, her preparation, or fact-finding phase, includes acquiring information and contextual background for the intended composition, selecting appropriate design principles for the subject, and becoming familiar with intellectual and emotive processes of creative problem solving.

For instance, preparation for *The Big Apple* (Figure B) involved a knowledge of New York City, of significant elements to be found in that context, such as the Brooklyn Bridge, high-rises, taxicabs, and riverboats. Ideation, or brainstorming of ideas, included exploring what elements were to be selected and combined into a creative composition, choosing appropriate analogies and symbols for effective communication, and determining colors and their proper combination for harmonious design and projection of the work. The integration of numerous ideas into a single, imaginative complex of beauty was achieved by Khatena's insightful grasp of the solution phase. Taken together, the idea and solution stages of the creative problem-solving process are directly related to Graham Wallas's (1926) incubation and illumination steps, such that generated ideas have the opportunity to simmer at the preconscious level to prepare the way for the "Aha!" experience of illumination. All at once, the totality of a bustling, variegated city emerged in original art, and a new work of beauty came alive.

## CONCLUSION

Creative imagination as a process and a teachable skill were discussed. This included the use of intellectual abilities and divergent thinking, as well as creative problem solving approaches in art composition with relevant illustration. In addition, principles derived from creative problem solving methodology as applied to art were illustrated in several creative works by Nelly Khatena. The next chapter further expands the discussion of the activity of creative imagination in art.

# 9

---

# Art Processed by Other Creative imagination Techniques

## OVERVIEW

I n this chapter, the discussion on using creative imagination techniques to facilitate production of original art compositions is expanded. Techniques used here are Synectics, analogy, and imagery and analogy in the reflective and problem-solving modes. The learner is taught to use these techniques using Nelly Khatena's artworks as an example.

## INTRODUCTION

We have seen how the creative imagination is set to work to produce the original using divergent thinking, and creative problem-solving processes. Other techniques that employ creative imagination to produce the new and unique in art include *Synectics, imagery and analogy,* and the evolutionary process of *synthesis-destructuring-restructuring.*

## SYNECTICS

*Synectics,* or mental activity involved in the combining of different and apparently irrelevant elements for artistic or technical invention, is another viable method of creative problem solving. W. J. J. Gordon (1966), the originator of this system, proposes conscious use of the preconscious to increase the probability of stating and solving problems creatively. According to him, understanding the psychological and emotional processes of creative activity is very important.

For successful invention to occur, the ability to tolerate and use attitudes, information, and observations not appearing to be relevant to the problem in hand, and the ability to play or sustain a childlike willingness to suspend adult disbelief are needed. In Synectics, three mental states are called into action:

1. play with words, meanings, and definition, which involves transposing a specific invention problem into a general word or statement;
2. play in pushing a fundamental law or basic scientific (or artistic) concept out of phase; and
3. play with metaphor.

To apply the first state to the visual arts, we need to substitute verbal for figural play and expression; states 2 and 3 remain the same.

## ANALOGICAL PROCESSES

Important to innovative problem solving are making the familiar *strange* and making the strange *familiar*, because breakthroughs depend on strange, new contexts by which to view familiar problems. However, familiar problems when viewed in a strange context may also lead to breakthroughs. That is to say, the creative process depends not only on presenting the old, familiar world in new ways but also on developing new contexts for viewing it. To successfully manipulate thinking for making the *familiar* appear *strange* or the *strange* appear *familiar*, it is essential to tap into four analogy mechanisms, each metaphorical in nature, their origin being the preconscious (Khatena, 1984). These analogical mechanisms are *personal, direct, fantasy*, and *symbolic* (Gordon, 1961).

### Personal Analogy

In *personal analogy*, a relationship is found between making a comparison and some other phenomenon familiar to a person. Suppose a girl wants others to know how thin she is without having to give a lengthy description. She may say in simile form "I'm as thin as a stick."

Here is an example of personal analogy that led to a scientific discovery. Friedrich Kekule von Stradonitz identified himself as a snake swallowing its tail. This led him to see the benzene molecule as a ring rather than a chain of carbon atoms.

*Crystal Gazing* (Figure 9.1), by Nelly Khatena, illustrates the use of personal analogy. The work presents the philosophy of an artist's perception of the universe and

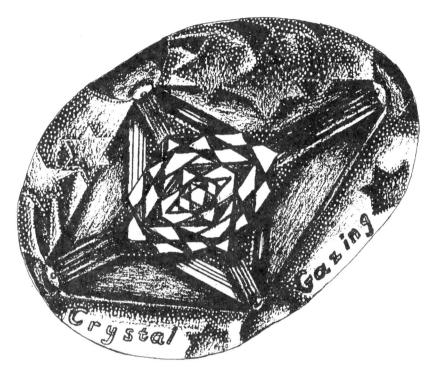

**Figure 9.1**   *Crystal Gazing.* Copyright © 1984 by Nelly Khatena. Reprinted by permission.

prefaces her "Egg Series." A crystal is presented in one plane sitting on several other planes of increasing size. Each plane is held up by projecting light rays radiating from each of four eye-like elements placed at each corner of the design. The rays create the multicolored lights of the crystal. Analogically, the crystal represents the universe upon which the artist gazes. Khatena makes the point that what is seen of the universe is through the egg-shaped eye. Circumscribed by an oval view of the universe, the artist sees the variety of its contents from different perspectives. With this, Khatena began her "Egg Series," such that each artwork that followed was but a specific projection of an infinitely productive universe.

### Direct Analogy

*Direct analogy* finds a relationship between two different phenomena without self-involvement. To produce a direct analogy, the "I" of the comparison above may become "Jean" and read "Jean is as thin as a stick." A direct *analogy*, which expresses contempt for corpulence, may be expressed in metaphor as "John is a pig." Direct analogy generates alternative points of view by association using comparison of parallel facts, knowledge, or technology.

Alexander Graham Bell's invention of the telephone taking life from his insightful grasp of the structure-function of the human ear serves as an example of this.

In terms of Nelly Khatena's art, *Fanfare* (Figure 7.1) is a good example of the use of direct analogy. The fan, being the basic image, finds direct comparison with the umbrella, hat, pagoda, and ginko.

### Fantasy Analogy

In *fantasy analogy*, the comparison subject or object must be imaginary. Myths, legends, allegories, and fairy tales are rich sources of imaginary materials for such comparisons. The literary mechanism for this is *allusion*.

Specific examples of allusions are the devil, Medusa, Pandora's Box, Ariel, a rainbow, the Garden of Eden, Sugar Candy Mountain, and Jekyll and Hyde.

Suppose you want to convey the information that someone is very evil. A well-known literary fantasy character is Hyde. Using this allusion, fantasy analogies such as "John is Hyde himself" or "Leonora's whispers stirred the Hyde in John" may be produced.

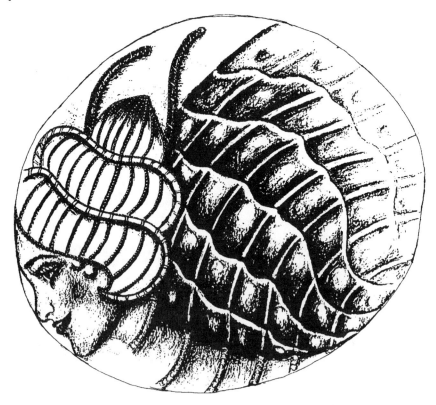

**Figure 9.2** *Metamorphosis.* Copyright © 1986 by Nelly Khatena. Reprinted by permission.

**Figure A** *Ginko.* Copyright © 1984 by Nelly Khatena. Reprinted by permission.

**Figure B** *The Big Apple.* Copyright © 1987 by Nelly Khatena. Reprinted by permission.

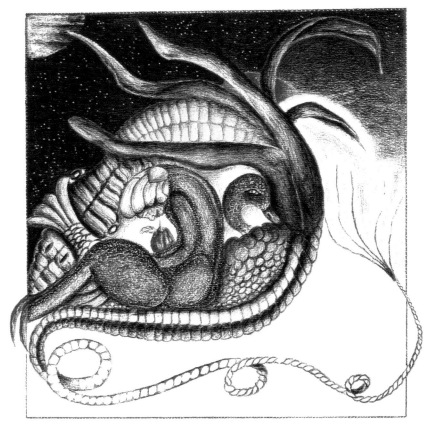

**Figure C** *Genesis*. Copyright © 1984 by Nelly Khatena. Reprinted by permission.

**Figure D** *Teacher in Space.* Copyright © 1986 by Nelly Khatena. Reprinted by permission.

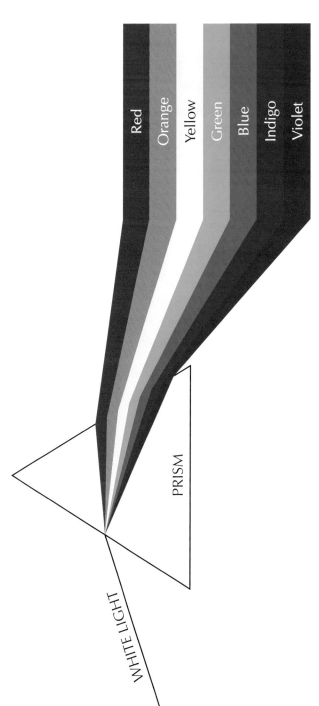

**Figure E**  White Light Refracted by a Prism.

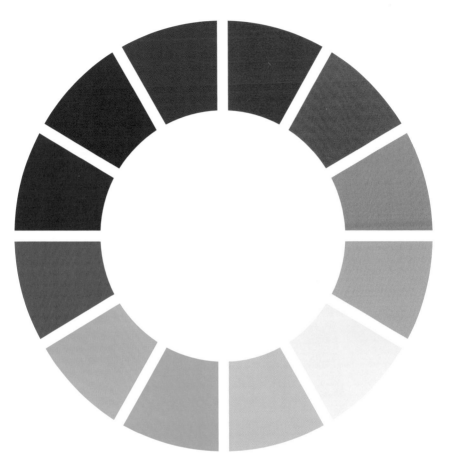

**Figure F**    The Color Wheel.

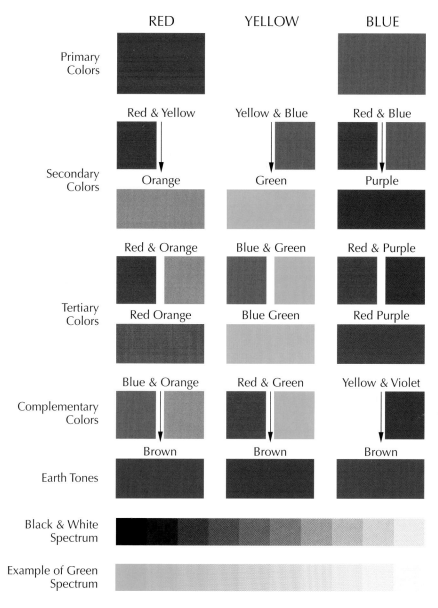

**Figure G** Combining Colors. Copyright © 1992 by Nelly Khatena. Reprinted by permission.

**Figure H**   Color Blossom. Copyright © 1984 by Nelly Khatena. Reprinted by permission.

Fantasy analogy also relates to wish fulfillment (Prince, 1975), such that all kinds of magical solutions may find expression in practical ways.

The problem of inventing a vaporproof closure for spacesuits is solved by imaging a skinny demon as a wire pulling together zipper-like springs imbedded in rubber illustrates this.

Nelly Khatena clearly utilizes fantasy analogy in her artwork entitled *Metamorphosis* (Figure 9.2). The art presents a woman wearing a headdress in the form of a beehive with snail-like antennae, and a body adorned in a shell-like skirt. *Metamorphosis* represents human integration and interrelationship with other natural forms. By implication, it also supports a theory of the sea origins of human life.

## Symbolic Analogy

In *symbolic analogy*, a sign or symbol is created for a phenomenon, comprising as many similar characteristics as the phenomenon itself. Should there be a need to describe someone as dependable, strong, stable, and consistent, without using too many words, one may select an animate or inanimate phenomenon that approximates possession of these qualities.

As an example, the Rock of Gibraltar can serve as a sign or symbol of the qualities possessed by the person in mind. Symbolic analogies such as "John is the Gibraltar of my life" or "Prudential is the Rock of insurance companies" may be created.

In the symbolic situation of sharks tearing at a marlin caught by an old fisherman in the novel *The Old Man and the Sea* (Hemingway, 1952), the fisherman is likened to the author, the marlin his literary productions, and the shark the critics who relentlessly tear away at his works so that nothing else remains but the marlin's skeletal structure, or the author's devastated works.

A superb example of symbolic analogy is found in Nelly Khatena's art composition entitled *Genesis* (Figure C, in the color insert in the center of this volume). The imagery of the work integrates various myths within a single picture (for example, Greco–Roman and Judaic–Christian) to *symbolize* the beginning of life where elements of destruction and death are also the origins of new beginnings and life. The biblically derived myth of Eve, apple, and reptile occupies a central position in the picture to signify the Janus face of life and death.

Behind the woman is a swan, an allusion to the form taken by the Greek deity Zeus (the Roman god Jove) as he prepares to mate with a woman. The ensuing sexual activity is poetically expressed in *Leda and the Swan*, composed in 1923 by W. B. Yates (1958). The juxtaposition of woman and swan subtly emphasizes propagation and continuance of life in Greco–Roman terms.

LEDA AND THE SWAN

A SUDDEN blow: the great wings beating still
Above the staggering girl, her thighs caressed
By the dark webs, her nape caught in his bill,
He holds her helpless breast upon his breast.

How can those terrified vague fingers push
The feathered glory from her loosening thighs?
And how can body, laid in that white rush,
But feel the strange heart beating where it lies?

A shudder in the loins engenders there
The broken wall, the burning roof and tower
And Agamemnon dead.
    Being so caught up,
So mastered by the brute of the air,
Did she put on his knowledge with his power
Before the indifferent beak could let her drop? (p. 241)

The symbolic significance of the fish, and the transformation of the reptilian body into the seed-like structure of corn, with peeled husk resembling human legs in motion delivering a reptile body, are indicative of fertility, procreation, and evolution. The further transformation of the reptile's tail into a piece of rope with frayed ends represents the continuous, open-ended nature of things and the outcome of human intervention and invention.

Day and night with the sun, moon, and stars provide the backdrop for the life and death imagery in the artwork. Taken together, the symbolic analogy and imagery of this artwork expresses the poetry of creation and its infinite life–death cycle.

## IMAGERY AND ANALOGY

*Analogy* making involves *imagery*, which can be described as mental pictures or images organized in meaningful patterns. One thing imagery does is make some sense of the world for the imagemaker.

The imagemaker is very much like an artist creating a perceived world. In the canvas of her mind, images appear as she reacts to the world she sees, and like the artist in the act of painting a picture, she gives organization and meaning to these images. How she depicts her world, what details she includes, the choices she makes of colors, the style she chooses, and the extent to which she allows her emotions to become involved are all dependent on her emotional and intellectual makeup and the creative, energizing forces working at the time.

Here, analogy is used to explain imagery compared to a painting. The mind is a canvas on which perceptions of the world are patterned. Imagery could have been compared to a painting with no attempt at elaboration. Instead , further details are added to the basic image—the individual is compared to an artist, whose mind is a canvas. Thus, by extending or elaborating the comparison, *images* are combined to make a more complex image pattern.

To put it in another way, "imagery is a painting on the canvas of one's mind." This is a *complex image pattern*. Simple and complex image patterns can be used in the act of comparison. The more highly imaginative a person is, the greater the tendency to use more *complex images*. Whenever personal, direct, fantasy, or symbolic analogies are created, imagery is used.

More often than not, analogies with complex image patterns tend to be more interesting and provocative than simple image patterns, as, for example, "Mary sings like a crow" when compared to "Mary sings like a featherless crow on a winter's day."

In Nelly Khatena's artwork, it is apt to compare the simple imagery of *Swanee* (Figure 6.21), a stylized reproduction of a swan, with the complex imagery of *The Big Apple* (Figure B, in the color insert), an exquisite artistic integration of the symbols of New York, such as:

the Brooklyn Bridge, its structure and suspension cables coalescing with the funnel and body of a riverboat;
the masks of comedy and tragedy representing drama and theater;
the repeat pattern of the black and yellow boxes of taxicabs in perpetual motion to indicate that the city never sleeps; and
the red apple on the top left-hand corner of the picture, representing the city itself.

It should be noted that emergent functions of analogy introduce meanings that go beyond the comparison object itself, such that the meaning "in a state of incompletion suggests the existence of others" (Ahsen, 1982, p. 233).

Nelly Khatena's art reflects the play impulse at work on analogical manipulation of generic motifs, which constitute the language of art, to transform everyday reality into art magic. Instances of this are to be found in her works already cited, and particularly illustrative of the use of analogy and symbol is *The Balance of Power* (Figure 7.3) or *Genesis* (Figure C, in the color insert).

### Reflective Imagery

*Imaging* is a mental processing of information in nonverbal or figural form that occurs freely or can be made to occur by planned experiences. In *reflective imaging*, a train of images may begin and continue when an individual is in a state of rest. This often happens just before a person falls asleep. Such imagery is known as *hypnogogic* to distinguish it from *hypnopompic imagery*, which occurs in a state of sleep at night or wake in the morning. In this twilight state brought about by the natural rhythm of sleep and wake, when control weakens, internal verbal chatter quietens, and attention to the external world is considerably lessened, images begin to flow quite freely, developing a life of their own. Take, for instance, Enid Blyton's explanation of how her imagery evolved for the composition of the *Noddy Stories* (cited in Stoney, 1974):

"I shut my eyes for a few minutes with my portable typewriter on my knee, I make my mind a blank and wait—and then, as clearly as I would see real children, my characters stand before me in my mind's eye...the story enacted almost as if I had a private cinema screen there...I don't know what is going to happen. I am in the happy position of being able to write a story and read it for the first time at one and the same moment.... Sometimes a character makes a joke, a really funny one that makes me laugh as I type it on my paper and I think "Well, I couldn't have thought of that myself in a hundred years!" and then I think "Well, who did think of it?" (p. 209)

*Autonomous imaging* such as this is creative. It is the precursor of poetic, dramatic, artistic, musical, and related composition. Images that occur have a life and meaning of their own, and may be loosely or closely strung together in a linear series, or may be organized in patterns and systems in structurally and functionally integrated wholes. We have only to compare *images* of the lyrical poem *Gather Ye Rose Buds While Ye May* (Robert Burns) and the imagery of the play *Othello* (William Shakespeare) to realize that one comprises of images beaded together like a necklace, while the other reflects images that interweave and evolve in situation and character dynamics to make the meaning of the play.

In art, *Swanee* (Figure 6.21) is an instance of connected images of a lyrical kind, its end result being the production of a stylized swan. *Genesis* (Figure C, in the color insert), described earlier in terms of symbolic analogy, can be said to be a good illustration of complex and profound imagery. Here, the artist integrates the imagery of various myths in a single picture to symbolize the beginning of life, in which elements of destruction and death are also the origins of new beginnings and life.

There is a need to make a distinction between experiencing images and imagery and recording them, which may or may not completely capture the flight of what often is very illusive information. What passes through the conscious mind are experiences from the preconscious, in the form of images transformed into the language of words, music, art, number, and the like. Recording of such images in some art form is most direct and requires the least change.

Communication of images via other language forms requires encoding it in the symbols of the relevant language. The recipient of the coded form of images, in decoding the symbolic form back to its image form, may or may not experience the original imaging. What also needs to be noted here is the encoding and decoding of images, which call for a fine interplay between the conscious and preconscious mind, and between the integrative functions of the logical-analytical-verbal left brain and the creative-insightful-nonverbal right brain functions (Jaynes, 1976; Ornstein, 1972). Images are primarily nonverbal and belong to the creative activity of the right brain.

### Problem-Solving Imagery

We have seen many creative geniuses of science testify that imagery for them was an important precursor to the solution of a problem, particularly occurring during incubation (for example, Einstein and the principle of relativity, Tesla and the principle of the rotating magnetic field, Kekule and the structure of the carbon ring).

*Incubation* and *illumination* are closely linked stages in creative problem-solving models (see Figure 5.2), especially overtly indicated by James Vargiu (1977) and Graham Wallas (1926).

As stages in creative problem-solving models (for example, Osborn–Parnes, Wallas, and Vargiu) pertain to imaging, the first, or preparation, stage is highly relevant and may take the form of reflective imagery. Imagery in the reflective mode is best suited to activity that finds expression in musical, artistic, or literary form.

For instance, before composing *Kubla Khan*, Samuel Taylor Coleridge (1956) had been working with various technical devices and reading Samuel Purchas's *Pilgrimage*. On falling asleep from the effects of an anodyne, a derivative of opium, taken to relieve him from "a slight indisposition," he experienced a vision in a dream that found poetic expression:

> In consequence of a slight indisposition, an anodyne had been prescribed, from the effects of which he fell asleep in his chair at the moment that he was reading the following sentence, or words of the same substance, in Purchas's *Pilgrimage:* "Here the Khan Kubla commanded a palace to be built, and a stately garden thereunto. And thus ten miles of fertile ground were inclosed with a wall." The author continued for about three hours in a profound sleep, at least of the external senses, during which time he has the most vivid confidence, that he could not have composed less than from two or three hundred lines; if that indeed can be called composition in which all the *images* rose up before him as *things*, with a parallel production of the correspondent expression without any sensation or consciousness of effort. On awaking he appeared to himself to have a distinct recollection of the whole, and taking his pen, ink and paper, instantly and eagerly wrote down the lines that are here preserved. (p. 181)

It must be noted that in problem-solving activity, the function of creative imagination involves intellectual abilities energized by emotive-motivational forces to produce creative imagery during incubation-illumination. However, imaging may also occur in the *preparation* stage, and must be associated with those creative thinking processes individuals use in creative imagination for the production of the original.

Not all input information is channeled to the brain via the senses in its direct or raw image form. There is much symbolically coded information that is received via the senses as well. The brain that is accustomed to decode such information into its imagery referents frequently does so. Such imagery becomes the raw materials that combine with other images drawn from storage, and as the creative imagination and its ability correlates act upon them, creative imagery is produced.

If no problem is involved, imagery takes its shape in the reflective mode, when it has life and direction of its own to find expression in a literary or artistic form. If images are associated with finding a solution to a problem, then they become the raw materials purposefully organized or reorganized by the creative imagination in various ways to achieve this end.

Incubation takes place without our conscious awareness and in conditions of rest or relaxation, or removal from direct conscious handling of the problem. Moments of inattention suddenly give way to the heightened experience of illumination, when peak imaging presents the solution to the problem.

## SYNTHESIS-DESTRUCTURING-RESTRUCTURING

The processes of *synthesis-destructuring-restructuring* is yet another manifestation of the creative imagination and its activity to produce the original. It is directly related to George Land's (1973, 1982) unifying principles of growth and transformation, drawn from nature's evolutionary processes of mutation and hybridization.

Growth is the key concept of Land's (1973) transformation theory. It is defined as "the process by which things become connected with each other and operate at higher levels of organization and complexity" (Land & Kenneally, 1977, p. 19) guiding all systems and subsystems. We know that the three stages of his theory relating to general principles of ordering are *accretive*, *replicative*, and *mutualistic*. These are all directional to transformation.

We shall recapitulate and elaborate Land's (1973) growth theory here. In the *accretive* stage, elements are drawn together until a pattern is established. If the pattern is satisfactory and directional to growth, reproduction or repetition of the order occurs. When the second or *replicative* stage has used up available resources or materials that easily fit the initial or modified patterns, it is ready for further growth. This growth is dependent on accommodating differences in the environment to bring about sharing relationships to establish the *mutualistic* stage in the growth sequence. Differences then become new sameness and direct the search for a new identity, when the process of disordering or destructuring of the pattern occurs and a new ordering or restructuring of the pattern follows, but at a higher level for the emergence of a *transformation*. The evolutionary cycle then repeats itself to bring about new transformations for continued growth at higher levels.

Transformation is where insight and invention occur, spurred by the catalytic effect of analogy and metaphor, and the resultant of a process that begins with synthesis, to be followed by destructuring and restructuring. This three-step transformation mechanism is integral to the evolutionary principles of mutation and hybridization.

Land's (1973) basic transformation concept is illustrated in the following example of creative activity by a child:

> If we look at the process of a child putting together a Tinker Toy, first we see exploration to discover a pattern—a simple box for example. Level two follows by adding other boxes, modified to accommodate different shapes and sizes. At the third stage all the pieces that can be easily made into boxes have been exhausted and the child begins to make rearrangement in order that the odd pieces that didn't fit well at first can become a part of the whole. This mutual stage of combining differences not only produces a new looking whole, but uses up the Tinker Toy. (Land & Kenneally, 1977, p. 23)

The process of synthesis-destructuring-restructuring, are other terms that can be used to describe Land's (1973) three growth stages relative to mental activity. It is important to the manifestation of creative imagination, often taking place with or without our knowledge or full awareness. Certain information or experiences are selected and ordered, or *synthesized*, to create a structure that hitherto did not exist. With the passing of time, dissatisfaction with the form sets in and needed change is perceived for new production. A readiness occurs for the structure to be pulled apart, or *destructured*, into its primary elements for the restructuring of something new, which may involve other elements of memory to produce the original.

A stimulating application of this three-step transformation mechanism can be found in Nelly Khatena's approach to simple art composition. She begins by making dots, dashes, arcs, circles, and related shapes of different sizes at random on a blank sheet of paper. The various elements are then synthesized by including transition lines until a meaningful image is created. Concentrating on the image provides leads to its further development. Either by physically erasing and adding new lines or mentally imaging possible changes, a new image (representational or abstract) emerges to be drawn as a picture. Perceived analogical relationships in the imaging-drawing process leads to the production of visual metaphor. The steps she takes leads to the final production of a picture of an insect, as illustrated in Figure 9.3.

Nelly Khatena says that one may not only use a pencil for such productive efforts, but also various kinds of paints and other materials that can be manipulated or sculptured. Once the picture is produced, it can be enhanced or embellished with additional relevant detail. The procedure can be repeated as often as desired for the composition of fascinating drawings, collages, and so on. Khatena provides another example of the process at work, calling it the *Magic of Intuitive Drawing* (Figure 9.4).

Here, a few dashes, curves, and small circles with tail extensions are drawn by her at random as a first step. In Step 2, joinings are made that produce an outline resem-

**Figure 9.3** Intuitive Drawing for Transformation. Copyright © 1983 by Nelly Khatena. Reprinted by permission.

STEP 1                                    STEP 3

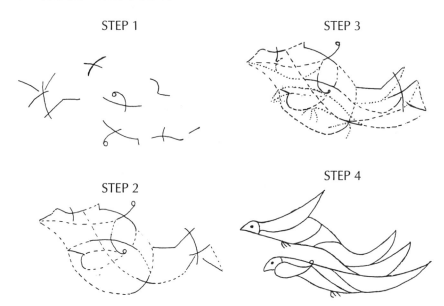

STEP 4

STEP 2

**Figure 9.4**   *The Magic of Intuitive Drawing.* Copyright © 1983 by Nelly Khatena. Reprinted by permission.

bling a bird figure (synthesis). Erasures and additions (restructuring) to the components of the form follow in Step 3, such that the figure assumes a more distinct bird silhouette, which in Step 4 becomes the figural representation of two birds. In this step-wise fashion, Khatena achieves transformation.

## CONCLUSION

Here, we have expanded the discussion of creative imagination to include the Synectics approach and analogical process, as well as imagery and analogy in the reflective and problem-solving modes applied to art production. In addition, we have shown how the evolutionary principle of systhesis, destructuring, and restructuring might be used to create works of art, with appropriate illustration by Nelly Khatena. Instruction on how these creative approaches may serve to produce artworks is discussed and practice exercises are given in Chapter 10.

# 10

## Instructional Application in Art

### OVERVIEW

This chapter describes instructional approaches that can be used to unleash creative imagination to produce works of art. It focuses attention on the environment as the major source of information received through the senses to become images that are symbolized as the language of art. The symbolized information is then processed by the creative imagination to produce beautiful and original artworks. In addition, works by Nelly Khatena are used as examples, followed by practice exercises.

### INTRODUCTION

Up to this point, much of the discussion has concerned itself with the nature and identification of creativity and art talent. In addition, the discussion has considered art, creative imagination and imagery, and the meaning and relationship of each of these terms, illustrated mainly by the selected works of an individual artist. Generic roots of the discussion take life from the Multidimensional Interactive Creative Imagination Imagery Model (Khatena, 1984), two dimensions of which, Environment and Individual, apply to the majority of artists in their act of art composition. Only a few artists of exceptional excellence find the *Cosmic* accessible in moments of heightened awareness, excitation, and vision.

Cosmic forces operate beyond the control of human beings generally and artists specifically and do not lend themselves to instructional purpose. Hence, we shall concern ourselves with factors relating to the Environment and Individual in our attempt to suggest some approaches that can be used to cultivate and nurture artistic talent.

## SOURCES OF INFORMATION

As has been discussed, we are dependent almost totally on the Environment for informational input, either in its raw or processed form. In its raw, or primary, form, information about the physical or sociocultural universe, received through our senses and nervous system, are recorded in the brain at first as images. Converted into language symbols, images are intellectually and emotively processed for communication. They find expression, for example, in the language of words, numbers, music, art, and dance. The outcomes of processed information also serve as input of environmental experience mediated by the individual. Received as language rather than raw experience, its modality is secondary rather than primary. Hence, an individual may engage in intellectual–emotive processing of both kinds of environmental experience.

In art, informational input begins, for example, with the sight of a bird in flight, the sound of the cascading waters of a waterfall, the taste of an apple, and the touch of a paintbrush. Everything in the environment provides information and usually is observed in more than one sense modality, such that we see/touch/taste an apple, see/hear a waterfall, or see/touch/hear a paintbrush. Common to these three sensory experiences is the use of the visual. We use our eyes primarily to gain information from the environment, though more than one sense may be involved.

The language of art is in the visual modality. Artists depend heavily on the use of their eyes not only to experience the environment, but also to artistically produce it. Thinking by an artist in the act of composition is primarily figural; communication is entirely visual. The outcomes of artistic communication—for example, paintings by Pablo Picasso (Rubin, 1980) or watercolors by Walter Inglis Anderson (Sugg, 1973)—also serve as informational input. Such input, communicated by others and received by an individual, is secondary in nature. The original, or primary, information from the environment, mediated by an artist's previously acquired information stored in memory, is processed to give new artistic outcomes. This is also a viable source of informational input for the recipient preparing to engage in artistic composition.

We are well aware that the richer and more complete the exposure of an individual to a variety of experiences, either in its primary or secondary forms, the better will be the informational base located in memory from which the individual can draw in the event of composition. An individual's exposure to experiences and events of the natural environment occurs by chance, unless intervention and planning by the sociocultural group incorporates and extends this to shape the individual in its likeness. Such intervention we call education, its function being to create learning situations so that the shaping process can be accelerated.

For the artist, images of external reality, derived from the environment and abstracted from natural phenomena, become symbolized in the brain as the alphabet of seven generic motifs. These motifs are the basic forms used in the act of art composition. Just as we combine various single letters of the alphabet into words, sentences, paragraphs, and longer pieces to produce prose or poetic works, the artist consciously or unconsciously combines one or more of these generic motifs to create various art forms. Composition in both the verbal and art language systems may aim at either reproducing experiences and events or imaginatively transforming them so that the various products that emerge lie along a continuum of reality and fantasy.

While these introductory remarks on the Environment provide artists with content for artistic composition, let us consider their significance in an educational context. This involves questions like: What can we do to lay the groundwork in formal learning settings that will enhance an individual's pursuit of artistic endeavors? What experiential focus can we give an individual to acquire information normally gained from the natural environment? What additional experiences can we provide a potential artist to establish and enhance a rich and comprehensive content base so essential to art composition?

A student of art needs to receive stimulation either directly from the natural environment or indirectly by simulation. For instance, there is much we can learn from the nature poet William Wordsworth. Nature to him was everything and he reflects its thrill in more poetic compositions than we can count. Included are such subjects as the excitement felt at the sight of a rainbow (1988, p. 171), beholding a sparrow's nest in a leafy shade (p. 156), watching a butterfly poised on a yellow flower (p. 172), a sweet highland girl (p. 191), and a chaste snowdrop as a venturous harbinger of spring (p. 575). Furthermore, in poeticizing about the influence of natural objects, Wordsworth observes that it calls forth and strengthens the imagination of a boy growing to adulthood (p. 113). *Tintern Abbey* is one of Wordsworth's most beautiful and telling poems. It captures the essences of nature and the effect they have on him, excerpts of which are presented as follows:

> *Five years have past; five summers with the length*
> *Of five long winters! and again I hear*
> *These waters, rolling from their mountain springs*
> *With a soft inland murmur.—Once again*
> *Do I behold these steep and lofty cliffs,*
> *That on a wild secluded scene impress*
> *Thoughts of more deep seclusion; and connect*
> *The landscape with the quiet of the sky...*
>           *...I cannot paint*
> *What then I was. The sounding cataract*
> *Haunted me like a passion: the tall rock,*
> *The mountain, and the deep and gloomy wood;*
> *Their colors and their forms, were then to me*
> *An appetite; a feeling and a love,*

*That had no need of a remoter charm,*
*By thought supplied, nor any interest*
*Unborrowed from the eye…*
                    *…Therefore am I still*
*A lover of the meadows and the woods,*
*And mountains; and of all that we behold*
*From the green earth; of all the mighty world*
*Of eye, and ear,—both what they half create*
*And what perceive; well pleased to recognize*
*In nature and the language of the sense,*
*The anchor of my purest thoughts, the nurse,*
*The guide, the guardian of my heart, and soul*
*Of all my moral being…* (p. 93)

Just as Wordsworth experienced nature directly and recollected the excitement in moments of tranquility to communicate in poetry, art students should expose themselves to natural surroundings, soaking up all that is around them to make the experience a part of their lives in preparation for artistic endeavor. Works of art may be done in the presence or absence of natural objects. If the purpose were to represent or reproduce experiences of nature, reliance would be on concurrent or remembered events. If the purpose were to compose, natural experiences would serve as the informational base to be acted upon by creative imagination for the transformation of nature into original art.

Quite often, we do not experience the natural environment completely and need to have our observations directed. For this to occur, it would be best to go to our natural surroundings and see for ourselves what exists around us. Not many of us notice the similarities between the structure of leaf veins and a branch or even the trunk of a tree with its branches. Nor do we easily see similarity among leaves, flower petals, and feathers. Ideally, actual examination of these objects would give the best benefit. That is to say a student of art may receive the experience directly by seeing and feeling the shape, structure, and texture of these objects in natural surroundings.

If such experience is unavailable, then exposure to artistic rendition of them is certainly the next best thing. Take, for example, the illustration of a leaf, flower petal, and feather in Figure 10.1. Instruction by reference to similar and different properties of the three objects can follow. Art students may then be encouraged to draw these specifics and even extend the drawings by applying them to other objects, such as a bird with wings composed of leaf-shaped feathers.

In attempting to make this point, Nelly Khatena synthesizes a leaf, flower petal, and feather in analogous relationship to produce a beautiful composition titled *Polly* (Figure 10.2). In terms of the language of art motifs, she uses patterns of the wave, straight line, circle, and zigzag to achieve this end. Other interesting features include the show of movement by the repetition of petals and leaves, and variety in unity by having petals, leaves, and feathers of similar shape aesthetically composed.

LEAF                    PETAL                        FEATHER

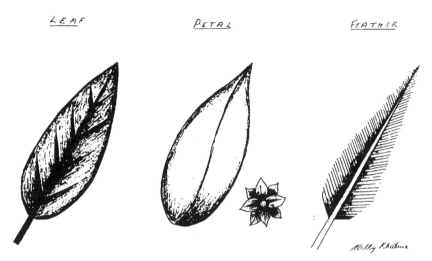

**Figure 10.1**   Related Properties of Natural Objects: Leaf, Flower Petal, and Feather. Copyright © 1983 by Nelly Khatena. Reprinted by permission.

**Figure 10.2**   *Polly.* Copyright © 1984 by Nelly Khatena. Reprinted by permission.

An art room should contain many specimens and illustrations, allowing the students to notice that, despite variety in nature, natural objects do have similarities. Comparisons should be made between different objects to bring out their common features, which, when abstracted and examined, assist in the categorization and simplification process. For example, attention can be called to a tree with its trunk and branches resembling the shape and structure of a leaf and its branched veins; or a river with its tributaries resembling the branching veins of a leaf; or a fish with its skeletal structure sharing similarity with the form and shape of a leaf. Opportunities should be given to art students to observe and discover the splendor of nature for artistic imitation.

A viable complement is processed information reaching the Individual as input, via the senses and neurophysiological pathways, to be recorded in the brain as images and their language referents. Such processed information is dependent on prior mediation by other individuals' interpretations of the external informational base of the Environment and communicating the results. For the artist, this takes the form of other works of art, dating back to primitive art, which illustrates the use of the seven generic motifs (Best-Maugard, 1952). Museums, books, and even travel guides or brochures are good sources of such information.

Generic motifs can be found in the art of such people as the Egyptians, Lake Dwellers, Assyrians, Chinese, Greek, early Britains, Persians, Hindus, Aztecs, Africans, American Indians, and Polynesians. In Chapter 6, we illustrated the use of generic motifs, showing Native American tapestry, shawls, and pottery; Chinese embroidery and ceramic decoration (Figure 6.20); and Panamanian art (Figure 6.21). Examples of the generic motifs can also be found in Greek frescos as far back as 1400 B.C., woodcuts of islanders in the South Pacific, African or American Indian ornaments, designs of body tattoos in Borneo, Mexican pottery, and 17th-century French textiles. The seven motifs can quite easily be found on the design of the king, queen, and jack of a deck of playing cards, something that has not varied much over the centuries (Figure 10.3)

**Figure 10.3**   Generic Motifs on Playing Cards.

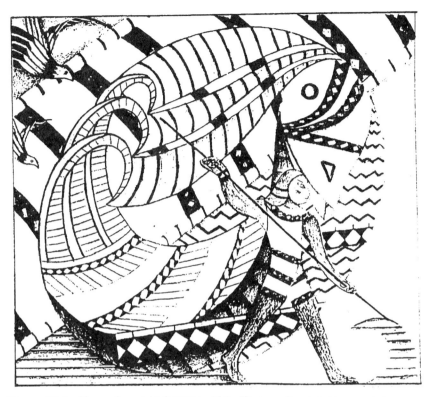

**Figure 10.4**   *Voyager.* Copyright © 1990 by Nelly Khatena. Reprinted by permission.

Another good example is to be found in Nelly Khatena's artwork entitled *Voyager* (Figure 10.4). The use of the seven generic motifs in this composition is quite evident. Note, for instance, the "straight lines" used to represent the sea, the masts and ribs of the boat, the various designs on the man's clothing, and the rod held in his hands; the circle for the eyes of the birds and carved figurehead of the bow; the wave pattern of the sails and the feathers of the bird; and the zigzags representing the waves and body design of the boat.

Art students may be given practice in the discovery or identification of the generic motifs present in as many of these works as feasible, followed by practice in combining the motifs in many and different ways to make new and more interesting designs. Furthermore, their observation can be sharpened by training them to observe current use of these motifs, for example, in designs of contemporary works of art, of buildings relative to their structure and ornamentation, and of furniture and fabric furnishings. They may then be encouraged to compose shapes that incorporate some generic motifs into a pleasing design, which can be applied to the construction of useful objects. In addition, they may be encouraged to try their hand in producing more advanced works, their aesthetic quality qualifying them as art.

## PROCESSING OF INFORMATION

Information by itself remains sterile until the artist breathes life into it. It comes to life through the intervention of the Individual. We have already indicated that when information reaches the brain through neurophysiological mechanisms, it is first recorded as images and subsequently symbolized as language. In the service of creative imagination are intellectual and emotive processes, which are activated by incoming information interacting with previous memory-stored information. The Individual, in the creative act, calls upon the intellect and emotion to process information in ways that lead to productive outcomes.

Creative brain activity is not confined to conscious handling of information alone, but relies on the sensitizing effects of the accessible preconscious and its evocative power for fantasy, examples of which were given earlier in two of Nelly Khatena's artworks, namely, *Metamorphosis* (Figure 9.2) and *Genesis* (Figure C, in the color insert in the center of this volume). Such activity can also be activated by altered states of consciousness, where facilitative agents include slow rhythmic breathing, hypnosis, drugs, and physical or mental exercise. The thinking that follows may either be deliberate or autonomous, depending upon whether the intellect (see Figure 8.1) is in the problem-solving or reflective mode.

Instruction, if it is to be effective, can profit by using these several mechanisms to achieve Individual productivity in the sciences and arts. Among these mechanisms are the sensory-imagery dimension, their language referents, the intellectual–emotive information processing capabilities, the several states of consciousness or awareness, and those conditions that facilitate the creative imagination to function optimally.

Innovative use of this knowledge can most certainly advance educational practice aimed at cultivating the creativity of most learners, including the student of art. Careful planning in developing each of these human propensities may be both generic and specific. The exercise of these functions will enhance the creative imagination of art students toward the production of works of meaning and beauty. To this end, let us consider how we may facilitate each of these dimensions of development, while recognizing that there will be some overlap among them.

## SENSE-IMAGE AND ART LANGUAGE

Whether we like it or not, we are exposed all the time to a variety of experiences as our senses come into contact with the environment. During our waking hours and in states of consciousness we may be aware of this, sometimes deliberately selecting experiences, at other times randomly experiencing all that is around us.

The rustle of wind in our backyard, the flight of a bluejay, the flow of water from a nearby brook, the sun setting on a lake, nightfall, the furry skin of a peach, the smell of an orange, a burst grape drenching the palate, and a million more. These provide information for the *senses* to be filtered and transmitted via neurophysiological pathways to the brain. Such information is attended to by one or more of our senses at a time so that we have images that are primarily visual, auditory, tactile, olfactory, gustatory, or any combination of them. That is why reexperiencing information in the auditory modality may call forth an image experience that was earlier recorded primarily by the visual sense, or active mental imagery of the experience rooted to several sense modalities. We call this experience cross-sensory.

Rosemary Gordon (1972) calls our attention to cross-sensory experience as the world of *synasthesia* when "visual images evoked sounds and tastes, and tones mixed up with colors and touch sensations" (p. 66). In a poem, Edgar Allan Poe (cited in Wilson, 1931) "hears" the approach of darkness. Elsewhere, Poe describes sensations accompanying death that illustrate *synasthesia*:

> Night arrived; and its shadows a heavy discomfort. It oppressed my limbs with the oppression of some dull weight, not unlike the distant reverberations of surf, but more continuous, which beginning with the first twilight, had grown in strength with the darkness. Suddenly lights were brought into the room...and *issuing from the flame of each lamp there flowed unbrokenly into my ears a strain of melodious monotone.* (emphasis added, p. 13)

The best *sensory* experiences we can give students of art are to be found in natural surroundings. Earlier in the chapter, we touched on the need and value of being in close touch with the natural environment. In keeping with this, art students can be taken out of the classroom to experience the natural wonders around them. A hike through the woods, for instance, with instructions to students to use all their senses to gain many experiences of life around them can be fascinating. Have them record these experiences using paper and pencil, camera, tape recorder or any other device that can capture the sensory experiences of the natural world. At times, encourage students to notice particularly what they see; at other times, have them attend to their natural surroundings with their ears. Perhaps have them notice how experiences strike them through several senses at a time, which in fact is a more common happening. Information of these sensory experiences can be recorded for future use.

Many an artist is dependent for inspiration by exposing themselves to nature; sometimes they seek new surroundings for stimulation to compose. Artists like Paul Gauguin, disgusted with the dubious delights of civilization, found the simple life of half-primitive natives in Tahiti the source of a lost paradise to be captured in original oil paintings. In Mississippi, Walter Inglis Anderson, well-known as the Islander, would visit Horn Island off the coast of Ocean Springs where, freed from human contact, he could be in touch with nature and the wildlife there. This solitary observation and communion led him to produce watercolor paintings of great beauty, reflecting experiences of sea, earth, and sky. In fact, many of the generic motifs we have talked about make up the language of his art.

The true artist often lives through sensory experiences of a selected environment, transforming these to images and language symbols of art. The experiences often thrills and the wonder that follows prepares the artist for composition. Recreating in tranquility the emotional state attending the acquisition of sense-image input, the artist becomes poised to put, for instance, on canvas or paper, an art transformation of the original experience.

The sociocultural universe also provides informational input to the senses for conversion into images and their symbolic language of art referents. The artist experiences people as individuals or in interactive groups engaged in the conduct of their daily sociocultural lives. Sharpening the observational powers of art students to behavior of people in all kinds of social and individual settings is the key to numerous experiential sources essential to designing and composing art. In the city, obvious places for such information can be found in streets, cafés, trains, underground stations, social or political meetings, or recreational gatherings. Conditions that people live in—such as poverty or wealth—are also significant sources of information.

Examples of paintings that illustrate the sociocultural context include: In *At Moulin Rouge* (1892), by Henri De Toulouse-Lautrec, oil on cardboard is used to depict a café scene in the Moulin Rouge with men and women grouped at tables, standing or walking; using pastel and gouache on canvas, Pablo Picasso, in *The Bullfight* (1900), illustrates bullfighters in a Barcelona arena preparing for an event; *The Potato Eaters* (1885), by Vincent Van Gogh, is an oil-on-canvas painting of five Dutch peasants sitting at a table peeling potatoes; and, David Alfarp Siqueiros's *Revolution Against the Dictatorship of Porfrio Diaz* (not dated) captures a scene of Mexican revolutionaries fighting for freedom in the early years of the 20th century in a mural painting of pyroxiline on masonite.

If we live in the city, we are bound to be exposed to such experiences. By alerting art students not only to observe, but also to make record of these numerous experiences, an informational or content base for art composition that gives art reality to actual circumstances can be established. The information, at first registered in the brain as images, is autonomously converted into art language symbols. By making art students aware of this image-language activity, we prepare the way for their recognition of generic motif components that make up almost any artwork. It is the act of composition that integrates the motif units into a meaningful aesthetic whole, personalized and vitalized by the artist's emotions and attitudes.

Art students can be exposed to works of art and given practice in reading and interpreting them. They may begin by noticing the image and art language referents, the compositional activity that bind all these elements together into a meaningful whole, and the life breathed into them to give uniqueness and strength of feeling, and value peculiar to the art creators. Individual perceptions of the works may be recorded in notebooks and later shared with others in discussion. Commonalty and differences may then be discerned and noted. Application of what has been learned may follow in a work shaped by individual students. Having sensitized art students in these ways, we may now turn them loose to compose. It is preferable to have students do this than to tell them to copy one of the works of a master in the hope that they will gain a feel for what it takes to produce a work of art. It puts them in the driver's seat, as it were.

Knowing the several ways one can use creative imagination and giving practice in their application will facilitate the process of art composition. These several approaches include the use of the "Structure of Intellect" model operations (see Figure 8.1), organized either in the reflective or creative problem-solving mode, its primary focus being divergent thinking, the evolutionary process of synthesis-destructuring-restructuring, and thinking by analogy and metaphor. Art students must become familiar not only with informational input forms, their symbolic conversion, and the mental-emotive activity involved in giving meaning and significance to the act of composition, but also with the processing mechanisms at work to make art happen.

## CONCLUSION

In this chapter, we have focused attention on the instructional aspects of creative imagination giving life to art production, and recognized that the major source of information lies in the environment. Information received through the senses become symbolized in the language of art and processed by the creative imagination to produce artworks of beauty. Illustrations of this were also given. Our discussion in the next chapter expands these concepts and emphasizes to individual dimension, including various approaches used by creative imagination to process and shape information into art.

# 11

## Producing Art Using Creative Imagination

### OVERVIEW

D iscussion in this chapter expands the concept of teachability of creative imagination to process images symbolized as generic motifs, the source of which is the environment via the senses, for the production of art. Here, stylized art composition is introduced and practice exercises are given in order to produce works of art. Attention is also given to processing generic motifs by using divergent thinking and synthesis-destructuring-restructuring to produce artworks, along with relevant illustration and practice exercises.

### INTRODUCTION

Information of a visual-figural nature, received by the brain as images and art language referents, have to be processed by one or more of several mental operations for art composition to occur. In Chapter 8 and Chapter 9, we identified these operations as functions of the creative imagination. They consist of divergent thinking and the organization of all five "Structure of Intellect" mental operations for creative problem solving, the process of synthesis-destructuring-restructuring for transformation, and analogical-metaphorical thinking.

These capabilities belong to the Individual dimension of the Multidimensional Interactive Creative Imagination Imagery Model (Khatena, 1984). Their use in creative composition of any kind is essential. In art, they are called into action whenever the production of creative works are intended. Artists use these approaches, very often without being aware that they are. The approaches are intuitively grasped and applied to serve the act of creative composition in art. However, we have been repeatedly reminded that awareness of the way potential creative imagination works only enhances our productive representation or creative production of the world around us. Alex F. Osborn (1963) has called this potential the "gold mine between our ears."

## STYLIZED ART COMPOSITION

We may not only interpret the world around us in our art compositions, but also select a certain style in which to represent it. The drawings that evolve from this are *stylized*. An example of stylized art can be found in the compositions by Pablo Picasso (Rubin, 1980), who was perhaps the first to introduce us to *cubism*. In this tradition, cubes and other geometrical shapes are used to modify realistic nature so that some features of it are recognizable in the art produced, or to discover symbolic values for realistic nature so as to produce art where natural forms are not recognizable. Stylized art of the latter kind is abstract art, its geometry being universal.

According to H. H. Arnason (1984), cubism may have paved the way to abstract art, though in itself it is not abstract art. By abstract art we mean art that is based on objects in the physical world that are modified or changed to emphasize content, bearing very slight resemblance to its original source (Preble & Preble, 1978). Examples of abstract art can be found in *art nouveau* paintings, where there is no recognizable subject matter, or where color patterns make the naturalistic subject disappear (Arnason, 1984).

Furthermore, to artist Kasimir Malevich must go the credit of extending abstract art from cubism roots to ultimate geometric simplification. According to Malevich, art had to be free of its visual object referent so that feeling gave meaning and significance to the work of art.

Vasily Kandinsky (1930) demonstrated that the existence of a painting could be entirely independent of reflection or imitation of the external world, be it figure, landscape, or still life. In the manner of free abstraction, he introduced regular shapes and straight or geometrically curving lines in several of his paintings. Later, this free form gave way to colored shapes bounded by hard edges, where he exhibited high levels of geometric control.

In themselves, geometrical shapes do not constitute art. Artists must breathe life into them by using creative imagination. Manipulated by creative imagination in any one of its several processing forms (for example, synthesis-destructuring-restructuring or analogy), geometrical shapes, their origins in generic motifs, become transformed into an art form.

**Figure 11.1** Design of Geometric Figures. Copyright © 1990 by Nelly Khatena. Reprinted by permission.

The triangle, square, rectangle, parallelogram, rhombus, pentagon, hexagon, circle, and oval are several of the most common geometrical shapes. Each of them may constitute the "mother" shape, within which may be drawn other shapes. If the oval were used to encompass other geometrical shapes, as Nelly Khatena demonstrated in Figure 11.1, separate geometrical figures may be designed, like the triangle, parallelogram, and hexagon.

Geometrical shapes can be combined to produce a picture design that includes various phenomena. Notice how Khatena has combined the shapes of a giraffe and horse, a spider hanging from its silken thread, a man flying a kite, birds in flight, a fish in water, and a plant with spreading leaves and flowers (Figure 11.2). This composition is an interesting example of an elementary form of stylized drawings in black and white, using several generic motifs organized as geometrical figures.

**Figure 11.2**   Generic Motifs in Stylized Drawing. Copyright © 1990 by Nelly Khatena. Reprinted by permission.

In another oval shape, Nelly Khatena composed another *stylized* drawing with a geometrical design, using several generic motifs that, when combined as triangles, circles, semicircles, and ovals, expressed themselves as heavenly bodies (sun, stars, planets), a manned rocket in outer space, and the alphabet. The occasion for this creative composition was the disastrous explosion in January 1986 of the space shuttle *Challenger*. The entire crew was killed, among them being Commander Frances R. "Dick" Scobee and teacher Christa McAuliffe. *Teacher in Space* (Figure D, in the color insert in the center of this volume), as Nelly Khatena titled the work, is a memorial to the ill-fated astronauts, their team, and their mission.

The composition illustrates not only a masterly use of generic motifs combined into a number of geometrical figures that convey a profound message, but also an exquisite use of embossment and color to create texture and contrast of light and dark. It further inserts letters of the alphabet to aesthetically name the work. The end result is a highly creative and beautiful work of art.

Another stylized work of great beauty by Nelly Khatena is *Reptile Walk* (Figure 11.3). Here, the artist uses generic motifs in freer geometrical form within an oval. Skillful connections of straight lines and curves results in the production of a visually pleasing movement of a coiled snake. Furthermore, the generic motifs of this design, processed by creative imagination, produces geometrical shapes so finely inte-

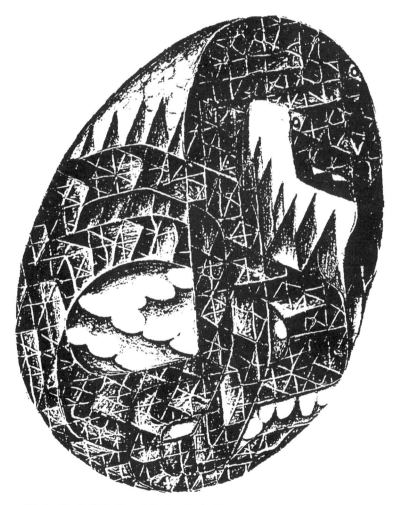

**Figure 11.3**   *Reptile Walk.* Copyright © 1984 by Nelly Khatena. Reprinted by permission.

grated that they are in themselves unobtrusive. The body of the snake spirals forth to become a geometric system. Zigzags on the body of the snake illustrate the texture of the snake's skin; and zigzags elsewhere represent trees and provide the setting for the snake. Oval flagstone-like shapes within the snake's winding body are eggs, representing fertility and continuance of life.

Although Nelly Khatena's preference has been for the oval or egg shape, in *Fergy* (Figure 11.4), she places the oval inside a rectangle, with meaningful content interplaying between the two. Generic motifs of straight lines, curves, and circles are finely combined to create a stylized design of a frog on a lily pad, with other smaller lilies floating on the water within the oval component of the design. The surrounding environment of plants provides the stylized version of a natural setting. All in all, it is a beautiful stylized composition.

Khatena's stylized artwork, where physical objects in geometric design are apparent, gave way to an abstract and a purer geometry. In the tradition of Malevich and Kandinsky, yet unique in her own conceptual and intuitive command of geometry, design, and color, she has produced many stylized artworks of an abstract nature that are universal in quality, as illustrated in Figure 11.5, Figure 11.6, and Figure 11.7).

**Figure 11.4** *Fergy.* Copyright © 1990 by Nelly Khatena. Reprinted by permission.

**Figure 11.5**   *Purple Blues.* Copyright © 1992 by Nelly Khatena. Reprinted by permission.

**Figure 11.6**   *Spinning Wheels.* Copyright © 1992 by Nelly Khatena. Reprinted by permission.

**Figure 11.7**   *Seeing Stars.* Copyright © 1992 by Nelly Khatena. Reprinted by permission.

## Practicing Stylized Drawing

Nelly Khatena's stylized and abstract works should provide examples for exploration for students of art. Here are a few practice exercises.

### Activity 1

Begin by choosing a geometric shape. Let's use an 8-inch square as an example. Mark off the horizontal and vertical sides of the square in 1/8-inch increments and draw the lines from side to side. Then draw diagonal lines, the first ones joining the four corners of the square. Using the 1/8-inch markings on the four sides of the square, make the remaining diagonals, each of which will be parallel to the first two, made by joining the four corners of the square. Now that you have some scaffolding in a square, you may join several points of intersection to make various geometrical shapes, such as a triangle, pentagon, parallelogram, or hexagon. Create a design in each geometrical shape that you have produced.

## Activity 2

Make a second square with similar scaffolding. Then go on to join points of intersection to produce various figures resembling a geometrical cat, bird, snake, and boy. In this way, you will be preparing for the design of stylized figures for the next set of connected drawings.

## Activity 3

Now, construct a third square. Once you have done this, consider using the stylized figures made in the second square to design a scene showing some relationship among them. Perhaps you can make these figures tell a story. This is the beginning of simple art composition that has visual narrative (Lowenfeld & Brittain, 1964).

## Activity 4

You may now experiment with other geometrical shapes. Suppose you choose an oval. Make guiding straight and curved lines within it. Using points of intersection, draw various geometrical shapes. You will notice that you now have greater flexibility in creating shapes.

## Activity 5

In this activity, try to visualize in your mind's eye how the shapes produced in Activity 4 may be designed into a related whole. When you are ready, begin drawing the interrelated geometric shapes into an interesting and unusual stylized composition. To help you in this activity, refer to the composition in Figure 11.3.

## Activity 6

Take the stylized composition of Activity 5 and select colors that will enhance and beautify it. Here, you may use as examples *Teacher in Space* (Figure D, in the color insert), *Reptile Walk* (Figure 11.3), and *Fergy* (Figure 11.4).

## Activity 7

Plan to advance your technique in the production of stylized art. This time, consider combining selected geometrical shapes into a composition with no recognizable features of realistic nature. Allow the principles of design to guide you as you proceed in your composition. Create a color scheme for your composition that will bring out its abstract beauty. Study Nelly Khatena's stylized art of purer geometry in Figure 11.5, Figure 11.6, and Figure 11.7.

Of course, geometrical shapes do not have to be used in stylized composition. Freehand drawing can be effectively used to combine one or more of the generic motifs into a work of art. The act of combining may involve the use of one or another of the creative thinking approaches given above and a discussion using the illustrations in Chapter 8 and Chapter 9. We provide some practice exercises on the use of creative imagination processes in the context of freehand drawing as we develop the discussion.

## DIVERGENT THINKING PROCESSING GENERIC MOTIFS

We have seen elsewhere how students can be taught to process information by using the "Structure of Intellect" operations generally and the divergent thinking operations specifically (Khatena, 1997a; Meeker, 1977/1980). Now let's look at the way divergent thinking can be used to creatively process information symbolized as generic motifs by freehand drawing. Divergent thinking, as has been previously described, is one of five hereditary-based mental operations of the "Structure of Intellect" model. It is primarily a creative processing mental tool. What it processes is information in its generic motif form.

To recapitulate, according to the "Structure of Intellect" model, information comes to us in four contents—figural, symbolic, semantic, and behavioral—that can be mentally organized as products in six different ways for communication. These are comprised of units, classes, relations, systems, transformations, and implications. Taken together, divergent thinking, with its content and product dimensions, comprise 24 ability cells, although Guilford (1973) used only 10 of them for constructing children's measures of divergent thinking (see Figure 2.3).

For purposes of art composition, information in *figural* form represent various environmental phenomena. Earlier examples included plant, animal, and human life; sun, moon, and stars; sky, earth, and sea; and earthquake, tornado, and hurricane. Their shapes are abstracted and *symbolically* represented as seven generic motifs: the spiral, circle, semicircle, two semicircles, wavy line, zigzag, and straight line.

Both forms of information may be processed by divergent thinking to produce creative outcomes in art from the simple to the complex. Either the figural or symbolic forms of information may be stored as images for this processing. That is why, in instructing art students, we need to make them aware of both the natural and symbolic generic motif forms. The *natural* form actually gives direct environmental experience, whereas the symbolic form gives indirect experience through the generic motifs that represent them.

The *behavioral* form of information, as has been indicated earlier, involves animal and human life forms, either as individuals or groups. It encompasses all kinds of sociocultural activity, which provides basic materials for many works of art. Again, behavioral information may be in its raw, observable form or in its generic motif or symbolized form. Take, for example, Nelly Khatena's composition entitled *Bamboo Bliss* (Figure 11.8).

Apart from the manipulation of generic motifs by divergent thinking to produce this artwork, depicted in a Chinese setting, note here the behavior of the three panda bears on the top left-hand corner of the work. The attention given by the mother to

**Figure 11.8** *Bamboo Bliss*. Copyright © 1987 by Nelly Khatena. Reprinted by permission.

her offspring appears to be the cause of the neglected father bear turning his back on them as if to move away.

The *semantic* dimension of information emerges when the figural, symbolic, and behavioral acquire meaning and significance. Together, these various dimensions of information provide the artist with the material needed for creative processing so that works of art can become the end result. It is now time to give art students some practice in the use of divergent thinking to process information within the confines of several ability cells of the "Structure of Intellect" model.

For our purposes, the operation of divergent thinking is used, as it processes figural information. To facilitate the creative process, the imaging approach is used, although nonimaging can also be used. We illustrate this by using four of the six operations shaded in the Divergent Thinking Operations section (Figure 11.9). These are *Divergent Production of a Figural Unit* (DFU), *Divergent Production of a Figural Relation* (DFR), *Divergent Production of a Figural System* (DFS), and *Divergent Production of a Figural Transformation* (DFT).

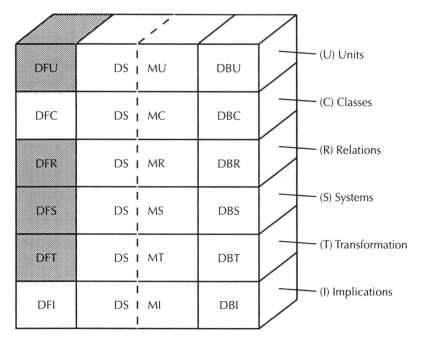

**Figure 11.9** Divergent Thinking Operations Applied to Content and Product. Reprinted by permission from Khatena, 1996.

## Practicing Divergent Thinking

### Activity 1. Divergent Production of a Figural Unit (DFU)
There are three generic motifs used here: two semicircles combined into an ellipse, two wavy lines joined together, and four straight lines combined to form a rectangle (Figure 11.10).

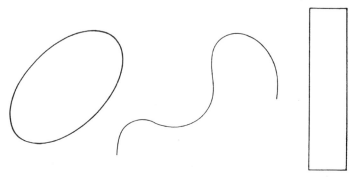

**Figure 11.10** Divergent Production of a Figural Unit. Copyright © 1983 by Nelly Khatena. Reprinted by permission.

Look at each motif, then shut your eyes and image each of them in turn. If you cannot image all three, open your eyes and take another look. Once again, shut your eyes and image the shapes. Take each one in turn and follow its line and curve until you know it well. When you have done this, let the shapes play about in your mind so that you see them combine and recombine in different ways. See them take shape to form various unusual and interesting pictures. When you are ready, open your eyes, and draw as many of them as you can so that each drawing includes all three shapes. When the drawing is completed, give it a title.

## Activity 2. Divergent Production of a Figural Relation (DFR)
Here are two wavy lines. Can you identify the relationship between them? They are in reverse of each other (Figure 11.11)

With your eyes open or closed, image this relationship in as many different ways as you can. When you are ready, draw as many of these images as you can showing this relationship.

## Activity 3. Divergent Production of a Figural System (DFS)
There are three generic motifs used here: a semicircle, a straight line, and two wavy lines combined to make an arch. These are presented as different movements of the arms, legs, or trunk in a dance (Figure 11.12).

Close your eyes and see these motifs of movement in your mind's eye. Play with them for a while. See them combine in various ways. Now let them take shape as a simple dance sequence. When you are ready, open your eyes and sketch out the image design you saw.

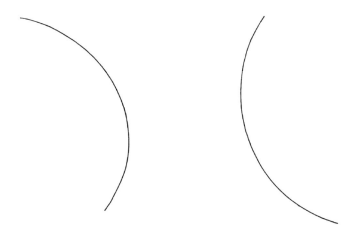

**Figure 11.11** Divergent Production of a Figural Relation. Copyright © 1983 by Nelly Khatena. Reprinted by permission.

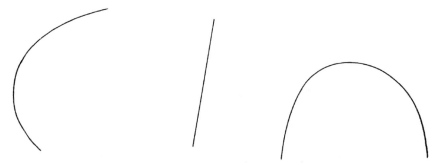

**Figure 11.12** Divergent Production of a Figural System. Copyright © 1983 by Nelly Khatena. Reprinted by permission.

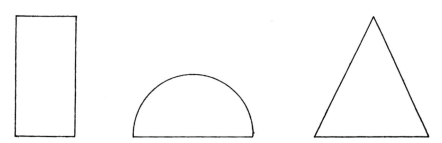

**Figure 11.13** Divergent Production of a Figural Transformation. Copyright © 1983 by Nelly Khatena. Reprinted by permission.

## Activity 4. Divergent Production of a Figural Transformation (DFT)

There are three shapes used here: a triangle, a semicircle, and a rectangle, produced from the generic motifs of straight line and semicircle (Figure 11.13).

Using each of these figures at least once, combine them to produce something unusual in your mind's eye. Image this with your eyes open or shut. With this mind play, you should now be seeing images of these figures come together to form an image design. When you are ready, draw the image composition you have created.

Perhaps at this stage of the practice, art students may be referred to the discussion in Chapter 8 on the use of divergent thinking in Nelly Khatena's composition entitled *Fanfare* (Figure 7.1). Here, the components of divergent thinking, referred to by Guilford (1973) as *ideational fluency, analogy fluency, expressional fluency, spontaneous flexibility, adaptive flexibility,* and *elaboration,* are shown in creative action in *Fanfare*.

Studying both the artwork and the processes involved in its creation, art students may be encouraged to experiment further with generic motifs and divergent production operations to compose art related to a subject of their own interest.

Some preparatory discussion on a subject, individually or in a group, and perhaps with illustration on the use of divergent production processing generic motifs within the subject content, either by the instructor or an advanced art student, would be most appropriate. Finer points of the application of design principles to the experimental work can also be discussed as the art lesson moves on.

## SYNTHESIS-DESTRUCTURING-RESTRUCTURING OF GENERIC MOTIFS

The operations of synthesis-destructuring-restructuring for transformation is a three-step process. First comes the combining of units of information to establish an identity. An order is established so that the object created can be recognized and named. A time comes when what was synthesized is no longer satisfying. A desire to make something else leads to the pulling apart of the elements making up the product. This operation is called *destructuring*. The elements freed are now ready for recombining, or *restructuring*, creating an object with a fresh identity and name. A transformation of the old order brings this about and the cycle is complete. As discussed in Chapters 2, 4, and 6, the process is evolutionary in nature and takes life from George Land's transformation theory, expounded in *Grow or Die* (1973).

The use of the above operations were illustrated in Nelly Khatena's artwork entitled *The Magic of Intuitive Drawing* (Figure 9.4), where several of the generic motifs were processed to become the figural representation of two birds. Advanced illustrations of synthesis-destructuring-restructuring for transformation are to be found in the various artworks by Nelly Khatena cited thus far and art students are encouraged to refer to them.

Another example of what can be done with just the wavy line motif drawn at random on a piece of paper is illustrated in Figure 9.3. Here, the three-step creative process was used to shape the motif of wavy lines into an insect. The transformation from line motif to insect was facilitated by concentrating or focusing on a form that took life from the act of physically joining, erasing, and adding new lines, mentally picturing possible changes. This creative activity was facilitated by the preconscious and memory retrieval functions.

### Practicing Synthesis-Destructuring-Restructuring

### Activity 1
Select three generic motifs, for example, the circle, wavy line, and zigzag. Of course, you can choose other generic motifs if you wish. Draw them on a piece of blank

paper. With nothing particularly in mind, add joining lines. Focus on what you now have and image it either with your eyes open or closed until the motifs take recognizable shape. This may make it necessary for some alterations to the initial joins. Open your eyes (if you have them closed) and erase previous connections and add new ones to shape them as close to the image you had as possible. What picture have you drawn?

### Activity 2

Suppose you decide you want to change the composition you created in Activity 1. On another blank sheet of paper, randomly draw the same three generic motifs and perhaps, if you wish, add a fourth. Look at the scattered motifs for a while, then shut your eyes and let these motifs play in your mind's eye until you get an idea of what you may want them to become. Open your eyes and begin making joins to them until some shape appears that you like. Concentrate on what else can be done to design it into an aesthetic piece. You can do this by erasing previously made marks and adding new ones. Once you reach a point of satisfaction with the drawing you have created, you can go on to embellish it.

### Activity 3

You are now ready for some advanced work on what you have learned and practiced. Take the two pictures you have created and perhaps add a couple more, either previously known to you or currently made. Image them interacting with one another. See how they relate together in a way that will allow you to draw a story about them. That is, make a visual narrative of these pictures. Place them in an environmental setting like the countryside or a town. When you are ready, begin drawing what you have imaged. Erase and add lines and spaces to improve your product. At this point you may consider adding color to your composition.

Refer once again to Nelly Khatena's artwork in previous chapters. Observe the generic motifs they contain and what the artist has done to them by using this aspect of her creative imagination. Perhaps you may now want to try to do a more ambitious work. Several trials will certainly lead you to produce a work of art, the processes of which are by now both intuitively and rationally known to you. Other works will surely follow that will give you great satisfaction and pride.

## CONCLUSION

We expanded the concept of teachability of information derived from the environment through the senses, converted to images and symbolized as generic motifs to be processed by creative imagination for art production. In addition, we introduced stylized art composition and gave practice in stylized drawing. Attention was also given to creative processing of generic motifs by the operations of synthesis, destructuring, and restructuring, and practice exercises were given. Chapter 12 further extends this to the use of analogy-metaphor mechanisms, and sounds and words as stimulating agents for creative imagination to engage in art composition.

# 12

## Analogy-Metaphor Making Art

### OVERVIEW

This chapter extends the use of creative imagination and analogy-metaphor mechanisms acting on generic motifs to produce art. Practice exercises are given to reach creativity of the preconscious. In addition, sounds and words are used to stimulate the creative imagination to evoke imagery and analogy-metaphor mechanisms to engage in art composition. Artworks by Nelly Khatena illustrate the processes at work, along with relevant instruction and practice exercises.

### INTRODUCTION

Yet another way creative imagination can be organized to process information for art production is by *analogy-metaphor*. This thinking mechanism operates on the principles of making the familiar *strange* or making the strange *familiar* (Gordon, 1966). The content of analogy-metaphor is primarily images that acquire language referents as a result of mind processing. Language referents of images facilitate thinking and make communication possible.

### ANALOGY-METAPHOR AND GENERIC MOTIFS

The alphabet of art, as we have described earlier, is comprised of generic motifs derived from the contours of natural phenomena. They symbolize the content of the universe. However, apart from serving as the art alphabet, generic motifs are by origin analogies. For instance, analogically the zigzag represents a mountain, the wavy line represents a river, the circle represents a moon, and the spiral represents a tornado. Many other examples can be found in Chapter 6.

A single motif may be found as the shape of many natural things. We have cited the wave motif, for instance, as the forming shape of a leaf, flower, feather, caterpillar, shell, duck, and rabbit (see Figure 6.24, Figure 6.25, and Figure 6.26). In this way, the wave motif becomes the basis for producing many analogies, such that there is similarity among the leaf, flower petal, and feather, although each object retains its difference.

The end result of thinking by analogy-metaphor is transformation of information. Take, for instance, *The Balance of Power* (Figure 7.3). Here, the expansion of analogy into many symbols is structured to represent the philosophical base of democratic governance in the United States. Another example is *The Big Apple* (Figure B, in the color insert in the center of this volume), where the expansion of analogy into many symbols is integrated to represent the exciting uniqueness of New York City. Both these works effect transformation of analogical units of information into complex provocative systems of thought.

Analogy-metaphor and imagery are powerful mechanisms of the creative imagination. They can be used to shape generic motifs—the alphabet of art—into works of beauty and originality. Artists do not necessarily have to be taught about these processes; these processes are activated whenever they become engaged in art composition. Students of art, however, are frequently not aware of the tools and magic of their trade. They sign up for courses and attend lessons in the expectation that their art teacher will equip them with the knowledge of these creative mechanisms and art language. This being the case, some guidelines for the acquisition and practice of analogy-metaphor and imagery may prove to be helpful. Consequently, we offer a few activities to help art students achieve this end.

## Practicing Making Analogies with Generic Motifs

### Activity 1

Start with generic motifs. Using each one of the seven motifs, draw several phenomena found in nature that they represent. In other words, draw analogies using the seven motifs below.

Spiral
Circle
Semicircle
Two Semicircles
Wavy Line
Zigzag
Straight Line

### Activity 2

Using the wavy line, think of several natural phenomena that look the same in some ways but are different in other ways (for example, wave, snake, and flower petal). Then draw them so that you bring out the wave pattern in each of them.

### Activity 3

Choose another generic motif (for example, a zigzag) and do the same with it. A few analogies containing the zigzag contour are mountain peaks and leaves. Think of other natural objects that have the zigzag in their composition and draw them.

### Activity 4

Now find four man-made products illustrating the spiral (for example, a staircase). These are also analogies. Draw them.

### Practicing Making Four Kinds of Analogies

#### Personal Analogy

You will remember that *Crystal Gazing* (Figure 9.1), by Nelly Khatena, was given as an example of the making of personal analogy in art and discussed in Chapter 9. In the making of personal analogy, artists must identify themselves with the comparison made between two or more things. The identification may be in the form of some association of self with the object of comparison, as in the illustration of oneself "as a cucumber in a bowl of ice" to indicate that one is as "cool as a cucumber." In the case of *Crystal Gazing*, the artist illustrates her philosophical perception of the universe.

### Activity 1

Suppose you want to focus a person's attention on the fact that you are an artist. With what can you compare yourself to bring out the fact that you can draw? It may be that you want to emphasize a part of your body for this purpose. See the comparison in your mind's eye for about a minute. When you are ready, try drawing then personal analogy that you imaged.

### Activity 2

Place several objects on a table before you (for example, a vase, a book, a pen, and a pair of spectacles). Imagine with your eyes closed that you are one of these objects and that you have the magical power to make the others come alive. Take a minute to do this. You decide that you will give your owner a surprise. Image for another minute the surprise you have for your owner. When you are ready, open your eyes and draw what you have seen in your mind's eye. Make sure that you are one of the characters in your visual narrative.

### Direct Analogy

The thinking mechanism of direct analogy is similar to that of personal analogy, except that there is no self-involvement in the comparison of two unlike things. In Chapter 9, we discussed this creative process and illustrated its operation by reference to Nelly Khatena's composition *Fanfare* (Figure 7.1). Using a fan as the basic image, the artist directly compares it to an umbrella, hat, pagoda, and ginko leaf.

In fact, the *Ginko* (Figure A, in the color insert) finds an analogous relationship between the ginko, or fan-shaped leaf, and a fan. Whereas *Fanfare* illustrates the principle of making the familiar *strange*, *Ginko* illustrates the principle of making the strange *familiar*.

Most of Nelly Khatena's artworks illustrate the use of direct analogy and should be referred to by the student of art. If we were to take the *Big Apple* (Figure B, in the color insert), for instance, we can easily find many examples of direct analogy (for example, black and white components of the border, which represent moving taxicabs in New York; the masks of tragedy and comedy representing the theater; and the cables of the Brooklyn Bridge and funnels of a riverboat representing one another).

### Activity 1

Compose a direct analogy by first imaging a rich man and a comparison object. When you are ready, draw the analogy.

### Activity 2

Think of the relationship between tall and short. Shut your eyes and in the next minute image several ways you can illustrate this relationship. When you are ready, open your eyes and draw the direct analogies you imaged.

### Activity 3

Elaborating from Activities 1 and 2, try integrating the drawings you have made so that they illustrate in visual narrative a message you wish to communicate. You may spend a minute or two to image this with your eyes shut before you begin your drawing. When you are ready, open your eyes and begin to draw the image you saw.

### Fantasy Analogy

We know that in fantasy analogy either the subject or object of comparison, or both, may be imaginary. An example of the use of fantasy analogy, cited earlier with explanation of this thinking mechanism, is *Metamorphosis* (Figure 9.2). This piece makes the point that human life has its origins in nonhuman, natural forms. The artist adorns the head and face of a woman with a beehive with snail-like antennae. The rest of her body is wrapped by a shell-like skirt. In this way, fantasy and reality are closely knit analogically.

Another example of fantasy analogy in art is illustrated by Nelly Khatena's work entitled *Strawberry Patch* (Figure 12.1). In this composition, a ladybug and a strawberry patch share a beautiful transformative relationship, such that what we see is not

**Figure 12.1**  *Strawberry Patch.* Copyright © 1987 by Nelly Khatena. Reprinted by permission.

the ladybug resting on a strawberry patch, but strawberries representing the spots on its back. Furthermore, the head, legs, and antennae of the ladybug resemble a bionic spaceship heading for the stars.

## Activity 1

Begin by using generic motifs. Suppose you select the wavy line. One analogy can be the drawing of a snake. Image the snake with your eyes shut. Play with the idea of making the snake into a mythological or fantasy creature. Give yourself between 1 and 2 minutes to let your images take a life of their own and run wild. When you are ready with a fantasy creature, open your eyes and draw this image. Once you have drawn it, you can, if you wish, use color to enhance the drawing.

## Activity 2

Recall an experience of anger or joy that you experienced sometime in the past. Shut your eyes and feel this experience once again. For the next 2 minutes, let your mind wander with the experience, allowing it to grow into an interesting and unusual image. When you are ready, open your eyes and draw the fantasy image you have created.

### Symbolic Analogy

In symbolic analogy, we compare representations of information to describe or explain relationships. We have already indicated in Chapter 9 how Ernest Hemingway depicted, in *The Old Man and the Sea* (1952), his critics as sharks tearing relentlessly at a marlin (representing his works) caught by an old fisherman (himself) while it was being towed to shore.

**Figure 12.2** *Fiery Wall.* Copyright © 1985 by Nelly Khatena. Reprinted by permission.

In art, *Genesis* (Figure C, in the color insert), composed by Nelly Khatena, was cited to illustrate the use of symbolic analogy, which integrates in a single picture the beginning of life, where elements of destruction are also the origins of new beginnings. Several of her other works have also been cited to illustrate the use of symbolic analogy, examples of which are the *Balance of Power* (Figure 7.3) and *The Big Apple* (Figure B, in the color insert). Another pertinent example of the use of symbolic analogy in art is the *Fiery Wall* (Figure 12.2). It is a composition that finds a symbolic relationship between a dragon and the Great Wall of China. Since the dragon is a mythological creature, the composition also shows the use of fantasy analogy.

## Activity 1

Begin with generic motifs and select those you think can be combined to illustrate forms that are life-giving, energizing, and beautiful. Close your eyes for a minute and image these taking shape. When you are ready, open your eyes and draw the symbolic analogies that you have experienced.

## Activity 2

Choose a country or state that is your birthplace or place of residence. List as many things as you can that represent or symbolize the chosen country or state.

Take each item in turn and think of what analogies you can make with them. Now sketch them on your pad.

Then look at each of the symbolic analogies that you sketched and think of how you can combine them into a composition that will visually communicate a meaningful and beautiful picture of your part of the country. When you have done this, enhance your composition with color.

### Practice in Reaching the Preconscious

Other ways to encourage and practice the use of analogies and imagery in art include devices that tap the preconscious. This area of brain power is the source of our creativity (Gowan, 1975) and a vast storehouse of imagery (Khatena, 1984). Among the devices that can serve as mind-openers, as suggested in the *Creative Imagination Imagery Actionbook* (Khatena, 1981b, p. 5), are:

| | |
|---|---|
| crystal ball | stage for dramatic productions |
| time machine | room with transparent walls |
| magic convertible | dream diary or journal |
| movie projector | Aladdin's lamp |

Any one of these devices can bring about a flow of images that include people, objects, ideas, events, or experiences in a natural or sociocultural setting. They can serve the art student as informational sources for compositions. Linked with the activity of constructive fantasy, the art student can find analogous relations among these imaged phenomena.

We have often heard the term *guided imagery*. This is imagery evoked by a teacher or leader giving instructions of a highly suggestive nature. The participant of such an experience is led through certain steps of relaxation and imaginary thought, during which time imagery activity occurs. The technique of guided imagery, which may use any one of the above devices, is most suitable for classroom imagery activity. Guided imagery sets the stage for *autonomous* or *spontaneous imagery*, when imagery takes a life of its own and is free flowing (Khatena, 1992).

Let us look at how we may use some of these devices to reach our creative source, the preconscious. Suppose we select the movie projector and time machine.

## Activity 1. Movie Projector

Think of your mind as a movie projector. You wish to see a movie, so sit down in a comfortable position for the experience. The movie you would like to see today takes you to the countryside, where there are people, farm animals, birds, woods in the background, and scattered flowers. (*Note:* If you wish, you may use a picture of a country setting or have a nature poem read to get your mind going.)

Close your eyes. The movie will last for 5 minutes. Start the projector. (*Note:* The art instructor may choose to guide the art student through this imaging activity with directions as to where to go and what to see, or the student may be left alone to image autonomously.)

The movie is almost over. Now you are back in the classroom. Open your eyes and tell us about what you have seen.

Now that you have shared some of the image experiences you have had, settle down to plan your composition. When you are ready, sketch the parts on a pad, paying attention to the way the parts can be made to relate to one another for the production of a whole picture.

You are now ready to use your creative imagination to compose a work of art. Consider what colors you will use to enhance your composition.

Do you notice what generic motifs you have used? Have you used any analogies? Is your composition conveying a message?

## Activity 2. Time Machine

You now have a very interesting activity ahead. This time, you will use transportation of a very special kind—a time machine. With it, you can take yourself to any time-space dimension, be it the past or the future.

Let's say you wish to go back 200 years to a location of your choice. When you are ready, shut your eyes and imagine you are in your time machine, about to manipulate the controls to get you to your destination. It takes 3 minutes to get there and back, so get the machine started. You are on your way and imaging the wonders before you as you make your journey.

You have arrived. Image getting out of your time machine to explore your surroundings. What do you see there? Who do you meet? What happens next? Experience the excitement of being in a different time and place.

It is time to return and you image getting into your machine and setting the controls for the return journey. You are once more traveling through the time-space dimension. *Image* that you are back in the room getting out of your machine and into your chair. Open your eyes and prepare to use your sketch pad.

Record on your pad as many image experiences you have had without necessarily attempting to integrate them into a composition.

When you are ready, use your creative imagination to plan a composition that will combine these separate sketched images into an aesthetic whole. Now that you have done this, add color to what you have created.

(*Note:* Other time-space dimensions may be selected for similar *guided imagery* activities.)

## USING SOUNDS TO STIMULATE ART COMPOSITION

Another viable approach to stimulate art students to compose is the use of sounds. A walk in the woods or country with a keen ear will soon alert us to many natural sounds that exist around us. The sound of a brook, a scurrying rodent, the twitter of birds, and the buzzing of bees are just a few examples of nature's music. We can only guess at the origin of other sounds. Walking along city streets will present to our ears man-made sounds, such as people jostling around or in conversation, schoolchildren yelling, cars in motion, a bottle breaking on the ground, and sounds in a market place of people selling their wares and housewives seeking the best buys.

### Activity 1
Here are a number of recorded sounds from the natural (or social) world. I am going to play them so as to create an atmosphere for your composition. You may use them to produce realistic art, or if you prefer, you may use them to create an imaginative composition. In either case, make yourselves comfortable and image the sounds that are being played back to you. Let your images wander until some interesting scene appears. If the scene appeals to you, then stop imaging and begin sketching it on your art pad.

You may use analogies to enhance your sketches as preparation for composition. This will lead you to design a total aesthetic art experience in which color will add to the harmony and beauty of the work.

### Activity 2
The first set of sounds you heard were recordings of the natural (or social) world around us. These provided you with experiences for Activity 1. The present set of sounds you are going to hear are those I creatively put together and recorded to challenge your imagination, and to stimulate you to compose.

Sit back comfortably, close your eyes, and listen to this recording. As you hear the sounds, see what images they conjure up and let your mind wander until they come together to make a meaningful scene.

As soon as you are ready, sketch the image experience you have just had on your pad.

Using your creative imagination, transform the sketch into a composition of beauty. Use analogies where you can to assist you. Then enhance the art piece with color.

## Making Your Own Image Pool

Recorded sounds, with narrative instructing students what to do, are also commercially available. One such recording is *Thinking Creatively with Sounds and Words* (Khatena & Torrance, 1998a). It is a measure of originality consisting of two components, Sounds and Images and Onomatopoeia and Images. These instruments, described in Chapter 2 as measures of the creative process, may also be used to stimulate the use of imagery and creative imagination.

Let us take, for instance, Sounds and Images. In Sounds and Images, three repetitions of a group of four recorded audio effects are presented, interspersed with narrated instructions. The instructions in effect force the listener to reject commonplace associations for freewheeling and imaginative ideas.

Sounds and Images presents both single and multiple sound sets, with encouragement from a narrator to use creative imagination in order to produce original images. It must be noted that responses produced by the listener are analogous to the sounds. However, the first reaction of the listener is to image and produce stereotyped or common responses. Considerable creative power is needed for a person to break away from the usual sequence of thought into an altogether different pattern of thought to produce original images and analogies. At this point, refer to the excerpt in Chapter 2 of the recorded narrative as given in the demonstration recording of Sounds and Images to recall the feel of the instrument.

We can use this instrument to stimulate art students to use their creative imagination in producing compositions. Although the narrative instructs the listener to write down their analogical responses, students may, if they wish, sketch the images they experience. Either way, the student will have created a pool of responses from which they can select for art composition.

## Activity 1

Here is a recording of sounds selected to stimulate you to use your creative imagination to produce original images and analogies. All you have to do is listen to the sounds and carefully follow the narrator's recorded instructions.

Close your eyes and useyour creative imagination to image each sound or set of sounds. Then open your eyes and write down (or sketch) the image on the response sheet before you. Work quickly, since the pause between one sound set and the next is brief.

The experience is meant to give you pleasure, so make yourself comfortable and get ready. Are you ready for the recording to begin? I am playing it now.

You now have a pool of images and analogies to select from for your art composition. Look them over to find one that has special meaning for you. Sit back and relax. Shut your eyes and begin to image it, letting it take shape (autonomous imaging) for the next minute or so. Open your eyes and draw on your sketch pad the image excursion, beginning with the one you chose.

Allowing your emotions to become involved, recall a recent experience of love (or hate, or anger, or jealousy). Look at what you have drawn. Now assume a comfortable position, shut your eyes, image the experience, and let it play in your mind. Let these images become meaningful to your emotional experience. See them advancing the action of the experience for the next few minutes.

When you are ready, open your eyes and draw your image activity on your sketch pad.

Look over the two sketches you have made. Using your creative imagination, figure out how you can expand them into a single artistic composition. When you have an idea of what you want to do, begin your composition. Then enhance the work with color.

## Activity 2

Go back to your response sheet with the pool of images and analogies. Look them over and choose two or three images you like best or find most meaningful. Close your eyes and play with these images in your mind until they come together in a meaningful way. When you are satisfied, open your eyes and sketch the experience.

Using analogies, modify the sketch into an artistic composition. You can then enhance it with color.

## Activity 3

Check the earlier sketches you made in Activities 1 and 2. Consider combining the ideas they illustrate with the new ones you have just created. Then sit back in a comfortable position, close your eyes, and imagine the coming together of the image experiences. Let the images combine and recombine in your mind. Give them the autonomy to wander for a few minutes. When you see an interesting scene emerging in your mind's eye and are ready to capture it on paper, open your eyes and begin composing the scene, adding color to it.

Some questions you might ask yourself should include: What generic motifs have I used? Have I expanded on the initial images and analogies I created in response to Sounds and Images? To what extent have I intuitively incorporated principles of design in my composition? Is it pleasing to the eye? Can it be at least considered a work of art?

## USING WORDS TO STIMULATE ART COMPOSITION

We have explained that information can reach us firsthand through direct environmental experience or secondhand through the communicated experience of others. Communication may take many language forms, like that of music, dance, and art. It can also take the form of words.

Words are symbolic representations of direct experience and can themselves paint scenes of good form and beauty. The imagery of good prose or poetry is evocative of mental pictures that approximately recreate the original experiences. Hence, hearing or reading the language of words may conjure mental images that artists can communicate through the language of art. Common to both language forms is imagery. By reaching the imagery level of experience, we place ourselves in a position to transpose information from one language system to another. This means that an artist listening to a verbal rendition of experience can transform its imagery for art communication.

We have already described the use of Sounds and Images to stimulate art production. The same may be done using Onomatopoeia and Images. This component of *Thinking Creatively with Sounds and Words* presents to the listener a recorded verbal sound or onomatopoeic stimuli with a narrator's encouragement to produce original responses. The reader should refer to a description of the instrument given in Chapter 2 and read the excerpt of the recorded narrative, as given in the demonstration record, to recall the feel of the instrument. Activities similar to those in Sounds and Images can be designed by the teacher or instructor to challenge art students to produce art pieces stimulated by word sounds of Onomatopoeia and Images.

Another approach would be to take a prose passage to stimulate the occurrence of images that could be imaginatively processed and transformed into a work of art. For instance, let us take an evocative description of a jungle night scene by a naturalist in Nicaragua (Belt, 1874/1954). In hearing or reading the following passage, we need to note and experience the imagery evoked by the prose.

### Activity 1. A Reading of a Prose Passage

NIGHT IN CENTRAL AMERICA

The night-world is very different from that of the day. Things that blink and hide from the light are all awake and astir when the sun goes down. Great spiders and scorpions prowl about, or take up advantageous positions where they expect their prey to pass. Cockroaches of all sizes, from that of one's finger to one's finger-nail stand with long quivering antennae, pictures of alert outlook, watching for their numerous foes, or scurry away as fast as their long legs can carry them; but if they come within reach of the great spider they are pounced upon in an instant, and with one convulsive kick give up the hopeless struggle.

### Activity 2. Transpose Prose to Art

Take a comfortable position, close your eyes, and listen to this prose passage as it is being read by your art teacher. Experience as many images as you can while the words are read.

Image yourself in this night world as an owl perched on the branch of a tree. What do you see happening below you?

Suppose you are a cockroach in this night scene. Image your observations and feelings.

If you instead prefer to take the role of a spider or scorpion, you may do so. What would this night scene mean to you? Image the events and feelings that follow your roleplaying of either the spider or scorpion.

Spend about 5 minutes with the images you have conjured and let them wander where they will.

When you are ready, open your eyes and sketch on your pad the *imagery* of the scene you experienced. As you do so, see how the images come together to form an artistic whole. Sketch this scene on your sketch pad.

Enhance your composition with color.

You should now ask yourself the following questions: Are there generic motifs in my work? Have I created any analogies? Does my composition follow the principles of design in art? Can my composition be considered a work of art?

All activities given are meant to stimulate you to use your creative imagination in art composition. They are suggestive of others that you may wish to attempt. You will no doubt find Nelly Khatena's artworks both inspirational and helpful to you in understanding the theoretical principles governing the function of creative imagination.

As appropriate, this artist's works were cited to support the discussion of art and the creative imagination as it progressed. One cannot help but notice the uniqueness and originality of Nelly Khatena's compositions. To observers generally, the works are in themselves beautiful; but to those who look at these art pieces with the intent to learn, they will reveal the wonder and magic of art composition.

## CONCLUSION

This chapter extended the activity of the creative imagination and the mechanisms of analogy and metaphor acting upon generic motifs to produce art. In addition, stimulation by sounds and words to evoke creative imagery and art production was also discussed. Proper illustration was given and instructional application was emphasized. Chapter 13 discusses the nature and role of the properties of color and texture, which are essential to art composition and expression.

# 13

---

# The Magic of Color

## OVERVIEW

This chapter discusses color and its relationship to light and value. Characteristics of color as it relates to the color wheel, its properties, harmony, effects on the eye, and how it affects the psyche also receive attention. This chapter also explores creating texture in art that is both actual and visual. Illustrations are also given as examples.

## INTRODUCTION

Much has been written on the subject of color from both perspectives of art and psychology (Birren, 1963; Gilbert & McCarter, 1988; Sargent, 1964). Color from the viewpoint of art is described in terms of visual elements, though some indication of its psychological effect has received notice. Most writers on color in art focus attention on its nature and function, bringing to the reader's notice the essential kinship that light and value share with color.

Any educated discussion on the topic of color must concern itself with its theoretical foundations and its properties tied to hue, value, and intensity. Furthermore, harmony of color, as well as its effects on the eye should also be given due consideration. How color affects emotions is clearly tied to the psyche and needs our attention from the perspective of physical properties that initiate emotional events and states.

Color has been touched upon earlier in this book. In Chapter 7, the topics of balance, harmony, and contrast in the use of colors are emphasized. Furthermore, color used to create stylized art, along with practice exercises, are given in Chapter 11. In Chapter 12, color to enhance analogy-metaphor production in art activities is also suggested. At this point, let us take a more careful look at some of the major visual elements that become involved in the use of color. Gaining an understanding of the nature and function of color will prepare art students for the development of essential skills. In this way, another set of tools for the creation of visual art will become acquired.

## LIGHT AND VALUE

There are two main visual elements that share kinship with color. These are light and value.

### Light

Realize that without light, color will not be perceived, as we see color because light exists. Take, for instance, the color of everything around us in daylight. When the sun goes down and we are in total darkness, everything around us cannot be distinguished beyond the color of black. For example, the view of a seaside scene at sunset, where waning orange gradually changes subdued blue-green waters to shades of blue, green, and gray; darkness overrides any semblance of color. Similarly, when light becomes extremely bright, differentiation of color is difficult. In photography, overexposed or underexposed film indicates the cause of undifferentiated elements in the picture, which is due to the varying activity of sunlight on the emulsion of the film.

Artists producing two-dimensional works of art sometimes create the semblance of illumination on their subjects. Natural or artificial light may be made to shine upon subjects evenly, illuminating them entirely on one side, casting shadows on the side not receiving light. Competent and creative manipulation of light by the artist can make a two-dimensional art piece appear to be three-dimensional and lifelike.

Color, seen in the presence of light, defines shape and mass. We discern the difference in a park, for instance, between trees, plants, and flowers, and between roadway and sky, all of which make a composite of a variety of colored objects. In a subjective work, an artist may project personal feelings or induce feelings in others by the use of color. Whereas the sum total of all colors of light combined will give white light, all colors of pigment when mixed will create a neutral color.

### Value

Another visual element of importance associated with light and color is value. By value, we mean the extent to which there is presence of lightness and darkness spread along a continuum. What better example than that which is given to us by nature, in the varying light intensities from day to night, or in the approach of a blanket of dark clouds as precursor to the occurrence of a storm. The relative brightness around us gradually changes to relative darkness.

Color is directly affected by the change in light values. If we were to plot these changes, a scale of extreme lightness to extreme darkness might be produced. Such a value scale would range from white to black, the former being the lightest and the latter darkest.

In art, the lighter values are referred to as high key, whereas the darker values are referred to as low key. Contrasts of light and dark are used in art to create the light and shadow of the natural world, and when used correctly, as observed, make a two-dimensional work of art seem three-dimensional and lifelike.

### Value in Black and White

Value may be in color or in black and white. If it were in color, it should be more easily distinguished than if it were in black and white. Take, for example, the black and white artwork entitled *Thirty Pieces of Silver* (Figure 13.1).

**Figure 13.1** *Thirty Pieces of Silver.* Copyright © 1987 by Nelly Khatena. Reprinted by permission.

*Thirty Pieces of Silver* utilizes a mixed media of pencil, pen, and paint. Its theme is the betrayal of Jesus by his disciple Judas for 30 pieces of silver. Many symbols are used to convey this information, stirring emotion and creating a mood. These include the crown of thorns with blood flowing down the forehead of the figure; the silver coins embossed with Caesar's head; the coins and flowing tears in hand directional to the crosses in the scene to the right; and the juxtaposition of plant or life and cross or death and afterlife.

In terms of value, we should notice the use of contrasts of light and dark created by the white of paper and the black of paint. Light coming from the right highlights the figure's forehead, right cheek, and tears, leaving the rest of the face in shadow. The light and dark pencil shading of coins offer compelling value contrast as well. Strong value contrast can be seen in the white of the palm leaves contiguous with the crown of thorns against a black background, or the crosses highlighting a gray-black background etched with lines for texture.

### Value in Color

Another example of the effects of value can be found in *Genesis* (Figure C, in the color insert in the center of this volume), where contrasts are created by the use of black and white and color. The black and white contrast directs attention to the compelling use of red in the serpent's tongue, sun, and apple, and in the changing hues of the serpent's head and body to effect a transformation that ends in a frayed rope-like tail. Furthermore, the texture of all the figures illustrates the masterly use of light and shade that turns a two-dimensional work to a three-dimensional work.

## COLOR

There is no doubt that art in color is more attractive and delightful. A case in point are the two works given as examples above to illustrate value (Figure 13.1 and Figure C). In real life, we are surrounded with color relative to light illumination. In comparison, objects in the least amount of light are dulled and almost indistinguishable from one another, except perhaps in their shape and mass. Although there is a place for artwork in black and white, and this is the case for pencil drawings, there is a significant preference for color. In fact, even passport photographs today are less likely to be done in black and white, and in many instances, laboratory facilities are less widely available to process black-and-white film.

We have already indicated the function of light in producing color. This is to say that no object possesses color in and of itself. Color is not intrinsic in an object, but is a function of light. A blue shirt is blue because the light that shines upon it absorbs all the colors of the light spectrum except blue.

In nature, we see a spectrum of colors in a rainbow, when sunlight shining on moisture in the air after a rainstorm has its light separated or refracted into different colors. The prism experiments of Sir Isaac Newton, the famous physicist and mathematician, have given us much of what we know today about color. Using a transparent glass with nonparallel sides, Newton passed a ray of sunlight through it and found that the ray broke up into different colors, much like what we see in a rainbow. To validate this finding, Newton reversed the process by recombining these colors into white light, or the original ray of sunlight, by having the refracted colors pass through a second prism. In this way, color as components of light was established (see Figure E, in the color insert).

Newton's prismatic separation of white light into colors of the rainbow can be linked with the color red-violet, not a color in the rainbow, but a transitional color, to make a circle of colors. This circle of colors is known as the color wheel. It should be noted, however, that there are several color systems, each providing a diagrammatic frame of reference designed to give standard identification attributes for all colors. One, called the Prang system, produced by a commercial house, is based on a two-dimensional concept presented as the color wheel. Two others are the Munsell and Oswald color systems.

The Munsell system applies to color in light as represented by an isosceles triangle, with the primary colors red, green, and blue-violet located at its angles. The Oswald system is a variation of the Munsell system, instead using the rhombus as its diagram. All three color systems concern themselves with the application of colors in pigment. A fuller discussion of these and other systems is presented in the books *Color: A Survey in Words and Pictures* (Birren, 1963) or *The Enjoyment and Use of Color* (Sargent, 1964).

## The Webster Color Wheel

Various theorists on color have constructed different color wheels. Here, we present the Webster system, which closely resembles Oswald's system, comprised of 12 hues to include the primary colors and their several combinations. The Webster color wheel is fairly standard and the version given should fit our purpose well (see Figure F, in the color insert).

The Webster color wheel consists of primary, secondary, tertiary, and complementary colors (see Figure G, in the color insert).

*Primary colors* are those that theoretically cannot be made by mixing colors. They are red, yellow, and blue (Row 1 in Figure G).

*Secondary* colors are those made by mixing two primary colors. They are orange, green, and violet (Rows 2 and 3 in Figure G).

*Tertiary colors* are produced by mixing a primary color with an adjacent color on the color wheel. For instance, mixing red with orange will create red-orange, or red with violet will make red-violet (Rows 4 and 5 in Figure G).

*Complementary colors* are produced by mixing colors directly opposite one another on the color wheel. For instance, mixing blue and its direct opposite, complementary orange, will give blue-orange; or red and its complement, green, will give red-green; or yellow and its complement, violet, will give yellow-violet (Row 6 in Figure G). In fact, these three mixtures blend to create earth tones (Row 7 in Figure G).

## Properties of Color

To add to the vocabulary of color are three color properties referred to as hue, value, and intensity.

*Hue* refers to the name of a color, as in any color on the color wheel (for example, yellow, blue, and red) or those produced by mixing them (for example, yellow-orange, blue-green, red-violet, or blue-orange). We have given examples of them in our description of primary, secondary, tertiary, and complementary colors.

*Value* has already been discussed as an element of light. It refers to relative lightness or darkness not only as it relates to white and black, but to a full range of most colors.

Color hues have normal value when the hue is what we expect it to be. For instance, proceeding down the color value scale of green, for example, we see the dark green hue getting lighter in value until it becomes light green. Moving in the opposite direction, the color value of light green moves toward dark green. If the color scale continued to move in either direction of normal green, white or black is eventually produced (Row 8 in Figure G). The full range of black to white hues is also given (Row 9 in Figure G).

It is interesting to observe, by reference to the Khatena version of the Webster Color Wheel (Figure F), that a comparison of these colors will indicate that relatively, yellow has the lightest value, whereas violet has the darkest value. Furthermore, according to the terminology of color theory, hues with lighter than normal value are referred to as tint and darker than normal value are referred to as shade. In the case of normal red to pink or dark red, the pinks are called *tints* of normal red, whereas darker reds are called *shades* of normal red (see Figure G).

*Intensity* refers to the relative purity of a given color. We sometimes use the words *chroma* or *saturation* for intensity. When we speak of the intensity of a color, we are talking about the value of a single color as it is produced in full strength, gradually receding into hues of lighter values with the use of white or subdued as it is grayed into darker values. The purer a color is, the lighter its intensity. A color may be lowered in intensity by adding to it combinations of white and black or its color complements (see Figure G).

## Color Harmony

Selection of colors by an artist for a work is usually intuitive. The way the colors are made to relate to one another in a work is referred to as *color harmony*. Various visual effects may be produced by the harmony of colors, which may be categorized as monochromatic, complementary, analogous, and triadic colors.

*Monochromatic harmony* involves the use of various hues of a single color in a composition, often distinguishable by their differences in value and intensity. A work of art that uses blue in monochromatic harmony would have all the hues of blue-violet, violet, and red-violet, or blue-green and green.

*Complementary harmony* involves the use of colors directly opposite one another, as found on the color wheel (for example, yellow and its complement violet).

*Analogous harmony* involves the combination of adjacent colors on the wheel (for example, yellow and its adjacent colors of yellow-orange and yellow-green).

*Triadic* harmony refers to the use of three colors that are of equal distance to one another on the color wheel (for example, red, yellow, and blue, or red-orange, yellow-green, and blue-violet).

By becoming aware that color harmony exists in a work of art, we may better understand why certain colors chosen by the artist work so well together. Harmony of color is essential to the beauty of a composition.

## A Geometry of Colors

The Webster Color Wheel or its Khatena version (Figure F) is generic to the composition of individual pieces of art in color. Abstracting various color combinations from this color wheel, an artist determines, as it were, an artistic DNA structure for each work created. A unique color identity results that distinguishes one composition from another.

Of particular relevance is a geometric composition by Nelly Khatena, entitled *Color Blossom* (Figure H, in the color insert). It effectively illustrates an application of the spectrum and properties of color. Geometric shapes are harmoniously combined in a creative design within an egg shape. Its beauty is enhanced by colors derived from the generic color wheel. The artist uses crayon pencils to build up secondary, tertiary, and complementary colors from primary colors with prismatic effect. In addition, this artwork adheres to the three color properties of hue, value, and intensity.

## An Artist's Color Wheel Guide

A very useful guide to the art student is the *Artist's Color Wheel*, published in 1989 by the Color Wheel Company, in West Covina, California. It not only effectively illustrates what we have already said about color and the color wheel so far, but also instructs us on various color combinations so as to produce a variety of color effects and to provide a key to color relationships or harmonies. If a slide rule, as an alternative to a hand calculator with mathematical functions, is a significant tool for the mathematician, the *Artist's Color Wheel* is an essential tool to the student artist struggling with the complexities of color. All information needed about color is included on three circular-printed softboard sheets, connected together in the center. A number of windows and relevant arrows provide specific information on how to manipulate color according to need.

## Color Effects on the Eye

Colors have different eye appeal, sometimes in themselves and sometimes in combination. Physiologically, the rods and cones of our eyes pick up different information for transmission to the brain via the optic nerve and its neurological pathways.

Our perception of color may be by simultaneous contrast, as when two complementary colors (for example, blue and its complement, orange) are placed next to each other. What this does is make each color more brilliant. For instance, if a blue is placed beside an orange, the blue will be a brighter blue, and the orange a brighter orange. The same will be the case for red and green or yellow and violet.

The phenomenon of an afterimage is another interesting characteristic of color. An afterimage can be created by staring at an object for about a minute and then looking away at a white wall, where an image of the object is perceived. In color, if a person stares at one or more colors of an artwork and then turns to look at a white surface, a faint afterimage, in complementary colors, can be seen.

Colors influence our perceptions of size and proximity, such that an object that is bright red, for instance, may appear to be larger and to come forward or advance, while a pale blue may appear to be smaller, becoming distant or receding.

Generally, colors of warmer hues, such as red, orange, and yellow, with high intensity and dark value can create the illusion of largeness and forward movement, whereas colors of cooler hues, such as blue or green, with low intensity and light values create the illusion of smallness and receding movement.

Eyes can also be used to combine colors, as when small patches of different colors are placed in close proximity. This blending or mixing of colors, normally done with light and pigment, can be created by an artist using the pointillism technique, developed by the painter George Seurat. This technique requires a careful and close arrangement of many tiny, colored dots. A closeup of such a painting will suggest a meaningless jumble of colored dots, but seen from a distance away, the dots assume a meaningful structure and arrangement of soft and subtle colors.

Another aspect is illusion, where an artist melds colors and structure to direct the viewer's eye to perceive one thing representing another. Take, for instance, *Strawberry Patch* (Figure 12.1), by Nelly Khatena, where a ladybug appearing to perch on a leafy bunch of strawberries is given the body of a strawberry, containing subtle color and object exchange of strawberries as decorative dots on its back. In addition, the branches of the strawberry bunch and the legs of the ladybug are made to look alike both in color and structure.

## Color Affecting the Psyche

Let us begin by recognizing that color in itself does not possess emotive qualities. Color belongs to the domain of the psyche, which serves as a trigger mechanism for emotional response. According to Faber Birren (1963), color has profound personal and emotional impact on human beings and therefore belongs not so much to the powers of the spectrum, but more to the psyche.

At the language level, colors have emotion inducing properties. Just like words, colors have factual and emotive meanings that release various psychologically based responses. Colors described by words have specific symbolic content, such that the word *red* is associated with anger ("I see red"), yellow with cowardice ("He is yellow"), blue with sadness ("I feel blue tonight"), green with envy ("She is green with envy") or jealousy ("the green-eyed monster"), and so on.

Furthermore, colors are associated with natural phenomena and temperature. For example, different shades of red are associated with fire and sun; various shades of blue relate to water; and white is associated with lifelessness or death, purity, snow, and ice. The list can go on to include such observations as red having the highest energy; blue as being cold, gloomy, and melancholy; violet or purple as being disquieting. However, let us reiterate that it is not the colors in themselves that necessarily have these qualities, but that they are perceived to have these effects on the psyche.

Another aspect of color, as related to the psyche, is that of mood. Birren (1963) indicates that, in the main, colors are associated with two moods. One mood may be brought about by the warm, active, and exciting qualities of red and its analogous hues. The other mood is related to the cool, passive, and calming qualities of blue, violet, and green. Areas of these hues tend to liven up or quieten down moods, whereby light colors are active and deep colors are passive.

Let us take, for instance, *Genesis* (Figure C, in the color insert) by Nelly Khatena. The color or hues of *Genesis* have strong psychical implications. Let us begin by noting the color combinations and contrasts that create the effects of procreation, life, death, and infinity. The serpent's red tongue, the red apple in the woman's lap, and the peeping red-orange sun actively energize and strikingly illuminate the image of the whole work. The juxtaposition of light and dark offers significant contrast between the light of day (sun) and night (stars) or darkness (night). The symbols of serpent with color and structural changes from yellow-gray to brilliant corn-yellow receding into the leglike husk strands of corn transformed to a yellow-gray rope, the maiden with red apple in hand, and gray-white fish and swan signify life, death, and infinity. The emotional response to *Genesis* is powerful and telling; the message of legend, imagery, and the preconscious are beautifully and effectively communicated by the masterful use of color and creative imagination.

Emotional responses can also be evoked by the use of black and white. Paul Zelanski and Mary Fisher (1984) suggest that a dark background with light images is evocative of fear, similar to nightmares in darkness. Furthermore, many dark areas in a work are suggestive of a bleak, lonely mood. The use of mid-values of black and white can create a sense of hopelessness or depression. Let us take another look at the pencil drawing of *Thirty Pieces of Silver* (Figure 13.1) and note the skillful use of black and white values, and the creative use of contrast in shade and highlight, which, in addition to the effect of the picture content, evokes powerful emotional response. Feelings of betrayal and grief are closely linked to the several images and symbols of the Christ story and strongly felt by the viewer.

## TEXTURE

We are surrounded by a textured environment. Everything in nature is textured in one way or another. We call this *actual texture*, which by definition is three dimensional and is primarily related to the sense of touch. Touch, aided by sight, can facilitate our perception of actual texture.

The sense of touch allows us to differentiate smooth from rough, fine from coarse, thick from thin, round from flat, and so on. It is through our tactile sense that we obtain information about various objects around us. These we register as images that assist us to have a feel for objects, even when they are absent (see Figure 4.1).

### Actual Texture in Art

Actual texture in art is especially evident in sculpture, crafts, and architecture. Sometimes paintings are made to have visual texture by the way artists lay the paint on the canvas, here thick, there thin. We can feel this by running our fingers on the painted canvas. Sometimes, even three-dimensional objects are attached to the canvas to communicate actual texture. However, by and large, textures in painting are visual.

Generally, painters and other artists of two-dimensional or flat surfaces can only simulate actual texture by various devices, thus creating illusions of the real. The eye perceives texture when objects or colors in a painting are closely spaced. What we see reminds us of stored tactile images of previous experience in the natural world.

### Visual Texture in Art

Texture can also be created by patterns. A pattern, for instance, is produced by highly repetitive motifs that are evenly spaced over an area of a work. The motifs can be any one or a comination of the *generic motifs*, as has been described in Chapter 6. *Ginko* (Figure A, in the color insert), for example, has the ginko leaf motif repeated within the confines of a fan, its shape resembling that of the ginko leaf. This motif intertwines with the wooden skeleton of the fan, creating visual texture.

Visual texture can be created by the way color is used and how color is built up by using several colors to achieve the desired color. Pencil crayons, especially a brand named Prismacolor (manufactured by Berol U.S.A), facilitates this process. Visual texture can also be obtained by contrasting colors and by varying their value and intensity. In addition, tools with a variety of edges can be used to emboss the flat surface of art paper to create different elevations of its surface as preparation for the coloring process that is to follow. Application of color on such a surface will effectively produce visual texture.

Many instances of visual texture can be found in Nelly Khatena's artworks. Among her works, presented in the color insert in this book, illustrating visual texture are: *Ginko* (Figure A), *The Big Apple* (Figure B), *Genesis* (Figure C), *Teacher in Space* (Figure D), and *Color Blossom* (Figure H). Five other works, presented here in black and white, also illustrating visual texture are: *Reptile Walk* (Figure 11.3), *Fergy* (Figure 11.4), *Purple Blues* (Figure 11.5), *Strawberry Patch* (Figure 12.1), and *Fiery Wall* (Figure 12.2). These 10 works of art are summarized below.

| ARTWORK | FIGURE NO./LETTER | COMMENTS ON TEXTURE |
|---|---|---|
| **Color** | | |
| *Ginko* | A | Three-dimensional colored objects such as ginko leaves and wooden fan; pattern in repetition of leaf motif and wooden skeleton of fan; color buildup of orange leaves; green and black wooden structure of fan; subtle shading of yellow and green leaves |
| *The Big Apple* | B | Three-dimensional colored objects such as bird, apple, and sun in red; contrasting straight and curved lines of bridge, skyscrapers, and roads; motif pattern repeated for perimeter; pencil crayon used to build to desired orange, blue, and black |
| *Genesis* | C | Scales of swan and fish; patterns of reptile body; red and other color effects; light and shade of day and night |
| *Teacher in Space* | D | Geometric; embossing; star against black background; color brilliance; shading |
| *Color Blossom* | H | Geometric shapes combined and repeated to form patterns; coloring and shading of patterns; building of colors; embossing and coloring the perimeter of egg-shaped design |
| **Black and White** | | |
| *Reptile Walk* | 11.3 | Etching lines and patterns on snake coils; contrasting shapes and colors |
| *Fergy* | 11.4 | Etching horizontal lines on lily pad; diagonal lines on lily and veins of leaves; embossing to produce scaly surface of frog's body; contrast of flat and horizontal surface; color contrasts red, yellow, and green |
| *Purple Blues* | 11.5 | Color contrast and shading; pyramids and stars produced; highlighting yellow and blue at center to produce movement |
| *Strawberry Patch* | 12.1 | Etching of veins of leaves embossing to produce strawberries and stars; highlighting and color contrasts; beetle resembling spaceship in flight |
| *Fiery Wall* | 12.2 | Etching for marks on top of wall; embossing to produce scales on dragon's body; transition from body to brick wall; three-dimensional effects; functional pattern on dragon's body; color contrasts of fiery breath and wall |

## CONCLUSION

Our discussion in this chapter focused on the nature and role of properties of color and texture, essential in art composition and expression. Illustrations were provided to give particular meaning and direction to students engaged in activities to produce works of art. The final chapter presents approaches that can be used to evaluate student art.

# 14

# Evaluating Student Artwork

## OVERVIEW

This chapter discusses approaches that can be used to evaluate student art. It deals with evaluating thinking abilities and subjective and objective methods of appraisal. In addition, it points to the lack of evaluation procedures for art and discusses approaches for student, peer, and teacher evaluation. Finally, the chapter provides two instruments for the appraisal of student art.

## INTRODUCTION

We now come to some much-needed direction for the appraisal of artworks, which both the student and educator can use. This chapter will discuss using evaluative thinking abilities, subjective and objective appraisal, lack of evaluation procedures in art, setting up appraisal criteria for art, appraisal approaches that include a diagnostic-facilitation model, development of an instrument for the appraisal of artworks produced, and use of the *Talent in the Arts* appraisal measure developed by David T. Morse and Joe Khatena (1991) for the purpose of grading student artworks by the teacher or for selection of student artworks for exhibition and award by a team of "expert" judges.

## EVALUATIVE THINKING ABILITIES

Guiding creative talent includes the dimension of appraisal that requires the use of evaluative thinking abilities. Appraisal or evaluation involves measurement and then judgment of the relative merits of a piece. At one level, evaluation refers to a set of abilities that is used to make judgments, and at another level, evaluation refers to a set of criteria against which are to be matched observations made about content and form of a product.

According to the "Structure of Intellect" model, evaluation is one of five hereditary-based intellectual operations (Guilford, 1967). In fact, creativity derives its meaning and significance from the use of evaluative thinking abilities. Any creative problem-solving activity requires the use of evaluation in the processing of information. A fine interplay, or "dynamic-delicate balance," between imagination and judgment is used at every stage of the creative problem-solving process, finally resulting in coherent insightful solutions (Guilford, 1977; Parnes & Biondi, 1975). This is to say that at every step of the creative process, the generation of "new" ideas is followed by evaluation.

The approach taken to judge a product or the process that gave life to the product is dependent upon whether creativity has been involved in the shaping operation. If the product or process is related to known information, as for instance in social studies, criteria for evaluation may be well known and tried, and judgment is made more easily. If the product or process is related to unknown information involving the use of creativity, criteria for evaluation is less straightforward and judgment may have to be suspended until new criteria are developed that represent the product or process concerned.

## SUBJECTIVE AND OBJECTIVE APPRAISAL

Judgment may range along a continuum of the subjective to the objective. This means that judgment, if subjective, may be at one end of the continuum totally determined by personal appraisal according to an internal frame of reference acquired over the years by exposure to experiences related to the item or product to be judged; and at the other end of the continuum, if objective, may be totally determined by commonly agreed guidelines as to how judgments are to be made. Between them lie many gradations of the subjective and objective, such that even in the event an objective judgment is made, a certain measure of subjectivity may enter into it. A case in point is scoring responses for originality, which, although dependent on a scoring guide objectively determined by the principle of statistical infrequency and relevance, still requires the use of some measure of subjective judgment to assign numerical values to responses.

Mathew Arnold (1955), a famous poet and literary critic, had indicated that appraisal of the originality of a work of art would depend on earlier works by the masters acclaimed as original. These works would serve as "touchstones" to the new works to be appraised. Such an approach, although to some extent objective, since it is dependent upon external criteria, is highly subjective and a matter of "taste." Progress was made by the measurement movement in creativity when originality guides were constructed based particularly on the principle of statistical infrequency and relevance (Guilford, 1967; Torrance, 1962).

## LACK OF EVALUATION PROCEDURES IN ART

Most measurement texts deal with the evaluation of school subjects as they relate to the 3 R's, social studies, and the sciences. Very little attention, if any, is given to the evaluation of the fine arts, and what instrumentation is available for the purpose generally relate to the identification of artistic talent (see, for example, Anastasi, 1982; Cronbach, 1960; Gerberich, Green, & Jorgensen, 1962). For instance, on the subject of measurement and evaluation in the fine arts, L. J. Cronbach and Raymond J. Gerberich, Harry A. Green, and Albert N. Jorgensen bring to our notice the use of the Meier Art Judgment Test (1940), the Graves Design Judgment Test (1941), and the Horn Art Aptitude Inventory (1951). All three measures aim at measuring art talent potential, with the first two quite dependent on the use of judgment. The third instrument presents exercises for sketching or doodling, and semi structured "springboards" as leads to evolving compositions and design, and as an indication of talent that may benefit from training. However, these authors, including Anne Anastasi, offer nothing tangible to measure, appraise, or evaluate art accomplishment.

An important contribution by Elliot W. Eisner (1985) reiterates the position that the arts are not to be considered just emotive forms aimed at providing satisfaction, but also essentially cognitive activities, its function being to appeal to the understanding. Furthermore, he suggests that such mental activity must be rooted in sensory forms of life. Eisner also makes the point that education cannot omit the fine arts generally and art specifically, for they form yet another dimension of literacy that enables students to secure deep and diverse forms of meanings in their lives. Educational equity, where students' accomplishments in the arts is properly recognized, is also advocated, for "education in the arts cultivates sensitive perception, develops insight, fosters imagination and places premium on well-crafted forms" (p. 212). In terms of evaluation, the first two statements have special relevance, namely, the thinking-emotive component and the sensory roots of mental activity involved in art production, both of which are consistent with the thesis of this book.

## APPRAISAL CRITERIA FOR ART

Identifying criteria for the appraisal of artworks will depend upon the nature and purpose of the assignment to be considered. Assignments may take many forms to include those given to art students as individuals or groups. Furthermore, assignments given may relate to ongoing semester art activity taken individually or as a whole, or as an end-of-semester activity. Whereas ongoing semester art activity, may be considered as developmental and closely connected to the teaching-learning process, end-of-semester art activity may be considered primarily as evaluative and grade-directed.

For the most part, teachers of art will have to develop their own instruments for measuring achievement, either stemming from graduated learning experiences in the classroom or from end products. For each learning experience leading to an assignment that is aimed to test the consequence of learning, the teacher will have certain objectives in mind, and these will vary from situation to situation. The objectives set will direct the formation of assessment criteria. Although it has been suggested (Gerberich, Green, & Jorgensen, 1962) that a few standardized measures are available for assessment of art achievement (for example, the Knauber Art Abilities Test [1932]), they are not altogether suitable for our purpose.

Both instruments purport to measure art abilities mainly related to the outcomes of art instruction. However, they may give some useful leads to the design of instrumentation suitable to the measurement of art achievement relative to the preparation suggested in our book. The most pertinent of these leads relate to drawing originality, understanding the proper use of light and shade, proportion, perspective, color, and pictorial composition. Reference is made to a memory-based, reproductive grasp of design and not to a proper understanding of the principles of design, which serves as the grammar and syntax of the language of art.

To establish criteria for appraisal of student artwork, we need to determine the purpose of the work and then draw from what has been said in the earlier chapters about art composition. The general categories to be used for the identification of appraisal criteria include: creative imagination and imagery energized by emotive processes; generic motifs as the alphabet of art; principles of design as the grammar and syntax of the language of art, which gives meaning to the composition; color and its related properties; and relevant informational content for effective communication. Put in another way, questions such as these can be asked: What is the work about? (factual aspects of the work), How does the artist convey the information? (emotive - technique), To whom is the work directed? (tone - technique), and Why is the information conveyed in this way? (intention).

This is consistent with G. T. Brommer and D. Kohl's (1988) discussion of the visual communication process, which, in analyzing a work of art, includes such areas as content, sensory properties, formal properties, technical properties, and expressive properties. In appraising a work of art, the evaluator may ask questions in the following areas:

**Content:** What is the work about? What is the major theme? Are there minor themes?

**Sensory properties:** Where are lines and shapes used? Are colors bright or dull? Which color dominates? Is texture evident?

**Formal properties:** Where is the center of interest or the area of emphasis? Are colors or shapes repeated? How is balance achieved and felt? What kinds of contrasts can you see? Is the work unified and how?

**Technical properties:** What medium is used? How large is it? How did the artist use the material to express his idea? Are the brushstrokes important to the work?

**Expressive properties:** How is mood established? What does the painting tell us? How did the artist feel about the subject? How do I feel about it? (p. 51)

## APPRAISAL APPROACHES

Evaluating works of art involves several types of criticisms: journalistic, pedagogical, and popular. Our concern here is of pedagogical criticism, which primarily involves the teacher and the artist. According to E. B. Feldman (1981):

> Pedagogical criticism is meant to advance the artistic and aesthetic maturity of students. It should not so much render judgments upon student work as enable them to make judgments themselves. The teacher of art should be capable to function as a critic of mature work; but for the pedagogic critic, professional work represents possibilities for stimulation and discussion; it should represent absolute goals of achievement.
>
> An important task of the teacher of art, one which involves his critical capacities, is the sensitive analysis and interpretation of a student's work to the student. From this criticism, the student learns how to shape and interpret, and gains insight into the direction of his own work. (p. 460)

This is consistent with the evaluation-diagnosis-facilitation model described above, which is both developmental and directional to the learning process in art. This means too that any kind of appraisal of student art should be dependent on purpose of assignment and criteria established to recognize their achievement.

There are several approaches that can be taken to appraise artworks. Among them are those that relate to self-evaluation, peer-evaluation, teacher-evaluation, and evaluation by several judges. The approach taken will depend upon the purpose of the evaluation.

*Self-evaluation* relates to an approach that involves appraisal by an individual. Often, a student that undertakes this needs to acquire the skill and relative detachment needed for the evaluation of a self-produced artwork. The criteria to be used will be the same, varying according to need. Some training in this area needs to be given to the art student. Perhaps the individual should learn to do the evaluation at first in the presence of other students in the class so that many can learn at one time from the experience. It should be the common practice for students to evaluate their own work before submitting them to the teacher for appraisal.

*Peer evaluation* can stem from practice in self-evaluation in the classroom. Having acquired some skill in evaluating their own artwork, students will then be in a position to comment on or critique the work of others. Such exercises will make students sensitive to the qualities that constitute good art, recognize flaws where they exist, and suggest improvements to the work. Discussion should be encouraged at every step of the way. In this way, an increased awareness will be built to facilitate the production of each student's artwork.

*Teacher evaluation* will at first involve the setting up of criteria applicable to particular art assignments that are to be evaluated. For this, the teacher will use the guidelines that have been suggested, illustrated later in this chapter. The teacher's task will be to judge relative quality of artworks presented by students both form the point of view of diagnosing strengths and weaknesses for continued learning during the semester, and for the assignment of grades as needed.

*Evaluation by judges* often relates to artworks submitted for competition. Such works are screened by a number of "experts" who designate the worthiness of the products for purposes of exhibition or awards. For instance, several judges will be asked to rate an artwork according to untutored judgment or preferably judgment based on set criteria so that there is common ground for agreement or disagreement. A composite of the ratings is then averaged to provide the quality index needed for the selection of the work. This should be followed by some computation to determine the level of interrater reliability to determine the authenticity and consistency of the judgments involved.

It is important to indicate the viable model of appraisal of "diagnosis and facilitation." Such a model assumes that a learner has something to learn along the way, that the learner can more effectively learn by acquiring an understanding of strengths and weaknesses of the work in hand, and that guidelines will be given for improvement to be followed by recognition of the progress made. If properly done, this can serve as a powerful developmental tool for the proper appraisal of students' artwork. The teacher needs to resist the ill effects of grading alone by incorporating this developmental tool as a part of the learning experience.

## APPRAISING STUDENT ART

As has been indicated, objectives need to be set to guide evaluation of student art. Information about suitable objectives can be found in the preceding chapters of this book, and these take life from such areas as informational content that is both factual and emotive, deriving its relevance from the physical and sociocultural universe; the language of art comprised of generic motifs as alphabets that can be combined to form various meaningful shapes and forms; design principles as the grammar and syntax of the language of art, which organize and formalize compositional aspects of a work for the sake of enhanced meaning and beauty; communication techniques involving the use of color, light, and shade, texture and related elements, and emotive-inducing properties of color; and creative processes that include creative-thinking abilities, imagery, creative imagination, symbol, illusion, analogy, and synthesis-destructuring-restructuring operations processing information, language, and technique. Furthermore, there needs to be an appraisal category that pulls all these together to provide a view of the quality of the work as a whole.

With these as guidelines, let us suggest the development of an instrument to be used for the appraisal of student artwork by self and others on the one hand, and for the purpose of diagnosis for facilitation on the other. One form the instrument can take follows.

## APPRAISAL RATING SCALE OF ARTWORK*

Student_____ Date _____

Name of artwork_____

*Directions:* Rate the artwork according to each of the following areas as best as you can. For each area, give a rating of 1 to 7 according to the following scale:

1   Below average
2   Somewhat below average
3   About average
4   Somewhat above average
5   Well above average
6   Very high
7   Outstanding

| Area | Explanation | Rating (circle one) |
|------|-------------|---------------------|
| Content | Factual information derived from the physical and sociocultural environment constituting the body of the work; emotive layers of meaning embedded in the work. | 1 2 3 4 5 6 7 |
| Language - art alphabet | Use of alphabet of art, consisting of generic motifs either singly or in combination, to make various shapes and forms. | 1 2 3 4 5 6 7 |
| Language - grammar and syntax | Meaningful organization or structuring of generic motifs by principles of design that contribute to parts or the whole of the artwork. | 1 2 3 4 5 6 7 |
| Communication | Use of perspective, color, light and shade, and texture; stirring emotional reactions by color; techniques of presentation; and technical accomplishments. | 1 2 3 4 5 6 7 |
| Creative process | Use of imagery and creative imagination, including flexibility, originality, elaboration, analogy, symbol, illusion, synthesis-destructuring-restructuring. | 1 2 3 4 5 6 7 |
| Overall | Take into account all these factors and any other pertinent attributes, to assign an overall rating for the artwork produced. | 1 2 3 4 5 6 7 |

* Reprinted by permission from Khatena, 1997.

An earlier developed instrument by David T. Morse and Joe Khatena (1991), entitled *Talent in the Arts*, is another instrument that may be used in the appraisal of student artwork in any area of the fine arts. The instrument is particularly useful for evaluations by teachers of end-of-semester performance in a course on art for grading purposes. It is also useful to judges who are engaged in making decisions on the selection of artworks for exhibitions and awards.

## TALENT IN THE ARTS*

Student_____ Talent area _____
Name of artwork_____ Date _____

*Directions:* Rate the student's talent in each of the following areas as best you can. You should rely upon your personal knowledge of the student's ability and potential as evidenced in coursework, personal accomplishment, performance, or presentation. Please choose your ratings for this student as relative to the ability of all students in your class or group. For each area, rate the student from 1 to 7 according to the following scale:

1  Below average: lower 20%
2  Somewhat below average: lower 40%
3  About average for all majors
4  Somewhat above average: upper 40%
5  Well above average: upper 25%
6  Very high: upper 10%
7  Outstanding: upper 5%

| Area | Explanation | Rating (circle one) |
|---|---|---|
| Expression | High degree of individuality or conveyance of feeling in the execution of work or performance. | 1 2 3 4 5 6 7 |
| Extension | Evidence of going beyond that which is taught; synthesizing of skills, styles or both in execution of a work or performance. | 1 2 3 4 5 6 7 |
| Judgment | The ability to evaluate critically one's own work or that of others; to identify what "works" and what does not in an art piece. | 1 2 3 4 5 6 7 |
| Composition | Understanding of design or composition principles well enough to compose or improvise a work to reflect a certain style, feeling, mood, or time period. | 1 2 3 4 5 6 7 |
| Overall | Combining all these factors and any other pertinent attributes, assign the student an overall creative ability/potential/ achievement rating. | 1 2 3 4 5 6 7 |

*Reprinted by permission from Morse and Khatena, 1991.

The numerical value of the ratings determined in these two evaluation scales will then provide the basis for determining grades. The assignment of grades will depend upon the grading system existing in the school concerned, which generally ranges from "A" (outstanding) to "F" (failing). By and large, grades assigned will not fall below a "D" (below average) for an artwork submitted for appraisal. A teacher may use ratings assigned to students for their ongoing semester artworks to compute a final grade at the end of the semester. Taken together, the two appraisal instruments should provide adequate information for the assignment of a final grade at the conclusion of the course.

## CONCLUSION

This final chapter gave attention to the evaluation of artworks. It discusses the importance of exercising evaluative thinking abilities and makes a distinction between subjective and objective appraisal. The point was made about the lack of evaluation procedures and the need for an appraisal system that establishes criteria to guide the exercise of sound judgment in appraising student art products. Two such approaches were presented for the purpose of such assessment.

This brings to an end our discussion on developing creative talent in art. We hope that parents and teachers engaged in the guidance of student art will find the discussion useful in guiding the creative imagination of young people to realize their full potential in composing and expressing themselves in the visual art form. By understanding the tools and processes involved in art composition, and by developing and guiding student acquisition of them, parents and teachers may prepare the way for the emergence of mature, original, and significant artworks.

# References

Abell, A. M. (1964). *Talks with great composers*. Garmisch-Partenkirchen, West Germany: E. Schroeder-Verlag.

Ahsen, A. (1982). Principles of imagery in art and literature. *Journal of Mental Imagery, 6*, 213–250

Anastasi, A. (1982). *Psychological testing* (5th ed.). New York: Macmillan.

Amabile, T. (1983). *The social psychology of creativity*. New York: Springer-Verlag.

Arieti, S. (1976). *Creativity: The magic synthesis*. New York: Basic Books.

Arnason, H. H. (1984). *History of modern art* (2nd ed.). Englewood Cliffs, NJ: Prentice-Hall.

Arnold, M. (1955). *Culture and anarchy*. Cambridge, England: Cambridge University Press.

Belt, T. (1954). Night in Central America. In R. Reeves (Ed.), *The writers way: An anthology of English prose*. London: Christophers. (From *A Naturalist in Nicaragua*, 1874, Abstract No. 39)

Benedict, R. (1935). *Patterns of culture*. London: Routledge & Kegan Paul.

Best-Maugard, A. (1952). *A method for creative design*. New York: Knopf. (Originally published 1926)

Birren, F. (1963). *Color: A survey in words and pictures*. New York: University Books.

Bowra, C. M. (1969). *The romantic imagination*. New York: Oxford University Press.

Brommer, G. T., & Kohl, D. (1988). *Discovering art history* (2nd ed.). Worcester, MA: Davis.

Clark, G. A., & Zimmerman, E. (1992). *Identification in the arts*. Storrs, CT: The National Research Center on the Gifted and Talented.

Coleridge, S. T. (1956). *Biographia literaria*. New York: E. P. Dutton. (Original work published 1817)

The Color Wheel Company. (1989). *Artist's Color Wheel*. West Covina, CA: Author.

Cronbach, L. J. (1960). *Essentials of psychological testing* (2nd ed.). New York: Harper & Row.

De Bono, E. (1970). *Lateral thinking*. New York: Basic Books.

De Bono, E. (1990). *Six thinking hats*. New York: HarperCollins.

De Bono, E. (1992). *Six action shoes*. New York: Fontana.

Dewey, J. (1910). *How we think*. Boston: D.C. Heath.

Dorn, C. M. (1976). The advanced placement program in studio art. *Gifted Child Quarterly, 20*, 450–458.

Durr, R. A. (1970). *Poetic vision and the psychedelic experience*. New York: Syracuse University Press.

Eccles, J. C. (1972). The physiology of imagination. In *Readings from Scientific American* (pp. 31–40). San Francisco: W. H. Freeman. (Original work published 1958)

Eisner, E. W. (1985). *The art of educational evaluation: A personal view.* Philadelphia: Falmer Press.

Feldman, E. B. (1981). *Varieties of visual experience* (2nd ed.). Englewood Cliffs, NJ: Prentice-Hall.

Freud, S. (1957). The ego and the id. In J. Rickman (Ed.), *A general selection from the works of Sigmund Freud.* New York: Doubleday Anchor. (Original work published 1923)

Gerberich, J. R., Green, H. A., & Jorgensen, A. N. (1962). *Measurement and evaluation in the modern school.* New York: David McKay.

Ghiselin, N. (Ed.). (1955). *The creative process.* Berkeley, CA: University of California Press.

Gilbert, R., & McCarter, W. (1988). *Living with art* (2nd ed.). New York: Alfred A. Knopf.

Gordon, R. (1972). A very private world. In P. W. Sheehan (Ed.), *The function of imagery* (pp. 63–80). New York: Academic Press.

Gordon, W. J. J. (1961). *Synectics: The development of creative capacity.* New York: Harper & Row.

Gowan, J. C. (1971). *The development of the creative individual.* San Diego, CA: Robert R. Knapp.

Gowan, J. C. (1974). *The development of the psychedelic individual.* Buffalo, NY: Creative Education Foundation.

Gowan, J. C. (1975). *Trans, art and creativity.* Buffalo, NY: Creative Education Foundation.

Gowan, J. C. (1977). Creative inspiration in composers. *Journal of Creative Behavior, 11,* 249–255.

Gowan, J.C. (1978). The role of imagination in the development of the creative individual. *Humanities, 24,* 209–225.

Gowan, J. C. (1980). *Operations of increasing order.* West Lake Village, CA: Author.

Grippen, V. B. (1933). A study of creative imagination in children by the contact procedure. *Psychological Monographs, 45,* 63–81.

Guilford, J. P. (1950). Creativity. *American Psychologist, 5,* 444–454.

Guilford, J. P. (1967). *The nature of human intelligence.* New York: McGraw-Hill.

Guilford, J. P. (1968). Creativity in the visual arts. In J. P. Guilford (Ed.), *Intelligence, creativity and their educational implications.* San Diego, CA: Robert R. Knapp.

Guilford, J. P. (1973). *Creativity tests for children.* Orange, CA: Sheridan Psychological Services.

Guilford, J. P. (1977). *Way beyond the I.Q.* Buffalo, NY: Creative Education Foundation.

Hamdon-Turner, C. (1981). *Maps of the mind.* New York: Collier.

Hemingway, E. (1952). *The old man and the sea.* New York: Charles Scribner's.

Horn, C. C. (1951). *Horn Art Aptitude Test.* Chicago: Stoelting.

Jaynes, J. (1976). *The origin of consciousness in the breakdown of the bicameral mind.* Boston: Houghton Mifflin.

Johnson, D. L. (1979). *Social interaction and creativity in communication systems.* Chicago: Stoelting.

Jung, C. G. (1921). Psychological types. In H. Read, M. Fordham, & G. Adler (Eds.), *Collected works of C.G. Jung* (Vol. 6). Princeton, NJ: Princeton University Press.

Kandinsky, W. (1930). *The art of spiritual harmony.* London: D. M. A.

Khatena, J. (1978a). *Creatively gifted child: Suggestions for parents and teachers.* New York: Vantage Press.

Khatena, J. (1978b). Identification and stimulation of creative imagination imagery. *Journal of Creative Behavior, 12,* 30–38.

Khatena, J. (1979). *Teaching gifted children to use creative imagination imagery.* Starkville, MS: Allan Associates.

Khatena, J. (1981a). *Images of the inward eye: Selected poems.* Starkville, MS: Allan Associates.

Khatena, J. (1981b). *Creative imagination imagery actionbook.* Starkville, MS: Allan Associates.

Khatena, J. (1982). *Educational psychology of the gifted.* New York: John Wiley.

Khatena, J. (1984). *Imagery and creative imagination.* Buffalo, NY: Bearly.

Khatena, J. (1992). *Gifted: Challenge and response for education.* Itasca, IL: F. E. Peacock.

Khatena, J. (1995). Creative imagination and imagery. *Gifted Education International, 10,* 123–130.

Khatena, J. (1997). *Appraisal Rating Scale for Art Work.* Unpublished manuscript, Mississippi State University, Mississippi State.

Khatena, J. (1999). *Enhancing creativity of gifted children: A guide for parents and teachers.* Cresskill, N J: Hampton Press.

Khatena, J., & Khatena, N. (1990). Metaphor motifs and creative imagination. *Metaphor and Symbolic Activity, 5,* 21–31.

Khatena, J., & Morse, D. T. (1994). *Manual for Khatena–Morse Multitalent Perception Inventory.* Bensenville, IL: Scholastic Testing Service.

Khatena, J., & Torrance, E. P. (1998a). *Thinking creatively with sounds and words: Norms-technical manual.* Bensenville, IL: Scholastic Testing Service. (Original work published 1973)

Khatena, J., & Torrance, E. P. (1998b). *Manual for Khatena–Torrance Creative Perception Inventory.* Bensenville, IL: Scholastic Testing Service. (Original work published 1976)

Khatena, N. (1995). Art and creative imagination. *Gifted Education International, 10,* 131–136.

Knauber, A. (1935). *Knauber Art Ability Test.* Unpublished manuscript.

Krishna, G. (1977). Prana: The traditional and the modern view. In J. White & S. Krippner (Ed.), *Future science.* New York: Anchor Books.

Land, G. (1973). *Grow or die: The unifying principle of transformation.* New York: Random House.

Land, G. (1982). *Forward to basics.* Buffalo, NY: D.O.K.

Land, G., & Kenneally, C. (1977). Creativity, reality and general systems: A personal viewpoint. *Journal of Creative Behavior, 11,* 12–35.

Lehman, H. C. (1953). *Age and achievement.* Princeton, NJ: Princeton University Press.

Lowenfield, V., & Brittain, W. L. (1964). *Creative and mental growth.* New York: Macmillan.

McKellar, P. (1957). *Imagination and thinking.* New York: Basic Books.

Meeker, M. N. (1980). *Structure of intellect sourcebooks.* Vida, OR: SOI Systems. (Originally published 1977)

Meier, N. C. (1940). *The Meier Art Tests: I, Art Judgement.* Ames, IA: Bureau of Educational Research, Iowa State University.

Morse, D. T., & Khatena, J. (1991). *Talent in the arts.* Unpublished manuscript, Mississippi State University, Mississippi State.

Ornstein, R. (1972). *The psychology of consciousness.* New York: Freeman.

Osborn, A. F. (1962). Developments in creative education. In S. J. Parnes & H. F. Harding (Eds.), *A source book for creative thinking* (pp. 20–29). New York: Charles Scribner's.

Osborn, A. F. (1963). *Applied imagination.* New York: Charles Scribner's.

Parnes, S. J. (1967). *Creative behavior guidebook.* New York: Charles Scribner's.

Parnes, S. J. (1981). *The magic of your mind.* Buffalo, NY: Creative Education Foundation.

Parnes, S. J. (1988). *Visionizing.* East Aurora, NY: D.O.K.

Parnes, S. J., & Biondi, A. M. (1975). Creative behavior: A delicate balance. *Journal of Creative Behavior, 9,* 149–158.

Parnes, S. J., Noller, R. B., & Biondi, A. M. (1977). *Creative actionbook.* New York: Charles Scribner's.

Preble, D. (1973). *Man creates art creates man.* San Francisco: Canfield Press.

Preble, D., & Preble, S. (1978). *Art forms.* New York: Canfield Press.

Prince, G. M. (1975). The mindspring theory. *Journal of Creative Behavior, 2,* 1–13.

Rhodes, M. (1961). An analysis of creativity. *Phi Delta Kappan, 42,* 305–310.

Rimm, S., & Davis, G. A. (1980). Five years of international research with GIFT: An instrument for the identification of creativity. *Journal of Creative Behavior, 14,* 35–46.

Rockenstein, Z. (1989). *Training the creative-intuitive mind.* Buffalo, NY: Bearly.

Rossman, J. (1931). *The psychology of the inventor* (Rev. ed.). Washington, DC: Inventors.

Rubin, W. (Ed.). (1980). *Pablo Picasso: A retrospective.* New York: Museum of Modern Art.

Rugg, H. (1963). *Imagination: An inquiry into the sources and conditions that stimulate creativity.* New York: Harper & Row.

Sargent, W. (1964). *The enjoyment and use of color.* New York: Dover.

Schaefer, C. E. (1970). *Biographical inventory creativity.* San Diego, CA: Educational and Industrial Testing Services.

Simonton, D. K. (1978). The eminent genius in history: The critical role of creative development. *Gifted Child Quarterly, 22,* 187–195.

Starkweather, E. K. (1971). Creativity research instruments designed for use with preschool children. *Journal of Creative Behavior, 5,* 245–255.

Stoney, B. (1974). *Enid Blyton: A biography.* London: Hodders & Stoughton.

Sugg, R., Jr. (Ed.). (1973). *The Horn Island logs of Walter Inglis Anderson.* Memphis, TN: Memphis State University Press.

Sullivan, H. S. (1953). *The interpersonal theory of psychiatry.* New York: W. W. Norton.

Taylor, C. W. (Ed). (1958). *The 1957 University of Utah research conference on the identification of creative talent.* Salt Lake City, UT: University of Utah Press.

Taylor, C. W., & Ellison, R. L. (1966). *Manual for alpha biographical inventory.* Unpublished manuscript, Institute for Behavioral Research in Creativity, Salt Lake City, UT.

Taylor, C. W., & Ellison, R. L. (1983). Searching for student talent resources relevant to all USOE types of giftedness. *Gifted Child Quarterly, 27,* 99–110.

Tillyard, E. M. W. (1956). *Shakespeare's history plays.* London: Chatto & Windus.

Tillyard, E. M. W. (1958). *The Elizabethan world picture.* London: Chatto & Windus.

Torrance, E. P. (1962). *Guiding creative talent.* Englewood Cliffs, NJ: Prentice-Hall.

Torrance, E. P. (1972). Can we teach children to think creatively? *Journal of Creative Behavior, 6,* 114–143.

Torrance, E. P. (1975). Asessing children, teachers and parents against the ideal child criterion. *Gifted Child Quarterly, 19,* 130–139.

Torrance, E. P. (1981). *Torrance Tests of Creative Thinking.* Bensenville, IL: Scholastic Testing Service. (Original work published 1966).

Torrance, E. P. (1987). Recent trends in teaching children and adults to think creatively. In S. G. Isaksen (Ed.), *Frontiers of creativity research* (pp. 204–215). Buffalo, NY: Bearly.

Torrance, E. P., Khatena, J., & Cunnington, B. F. (1998). *Thinking creatively with sounds and words.* Bensenville, IL: Scholastic Testing Service. (Original work published 1973)

Vargiu, J. (1977). Creativity: The purposeful imagination. *Synthesis, 3-4,* 17–53.

Wallace, G. (1926). *The art of thought.* London: C. A. Watts.

Wallach, M. A., & Kogan, N. (1965). *Modes of thinking in young children.* New York: Holt, Rinehart & Winston.

Wallas, G. (1926). *The art of thought.* London: C. A. Watts.

*Webster's New World Dictionary of the American Language* (College ed.). (1980). New York: World.

White, J., & Krippner, S. (Eds.). (1977). *Future science: Life energies and the physics of paranormal phenomena.* New York: Anchor Books.

Wilson, B., & Wilson, M. (1976). Visual narrative and artistically gifted. *Gifted Child Quarterly*, *20*, 432–447.

Wilson, E. (1931). *Axel's castle: A study of the imaginative literature.* New York: Charles Scribner's.

Wordsworth, W. (1988). *The complete works of William Wordsworth.* London: Macmillan.

Yates, W. B. (1958). *Complete works of William B. Yates.* London: Macmillan.

Zelanski, P., & Fisher, M. P. (1984). *Design principles and problems.* New York: Holt, Rinehart and Winston.

# Author Index

**A**

Abell, A. M., 49, 55, *181*
Ahsen, A., 109, *181*
Amabile, T., 5, *181*
Anastasi, A., 173, *181*
Arieti, S., 4, 45, 46, 62, *181*
Arnason, H. H., 128, *181*
Arnold, M., 42, 172, *181*

**B**

Belt, T., 156, *181*
Benedict, R., 45, *181*
Best-Maugard, A., 56, 70, 84, 120, *181*
Biondi, A. M., 94, 100, 172, *183*
Birren, F., 159, 163, 166, *181*
Bowra, C. M., 49, 57, *181*
Brittain, W. L., 34, 135, *183*
Brommer, G. T., 62, 174, *181*

**C**

Clark, G. A., 37, *181*
Coleridge, S. T., 24, 49, 55, 57, 111, *181*
Cronbach, L. J., 173, *181*
Cunnington, B. F., 22, *184*

**D**

Davis, G. A., 29, *183*
De Bono, E., 4, 6, *181*
Dewey, J., 95, 96, *181*
Dorn, C. M., 35, 36, *181*
Durr, R. A., 54, 55, *181*

**E**

Eccles, J. C., 57, 60, *182*
Eisner, E. W., 173, *182*

Ellison, R. L., 29, 31, *184*

**F**

Feldman, E. B., 62, 175, *182*
Fisher, M. P., 167, *185*
Freud, S., 47, *182*

**G**

Gerberich, J. R., 173, 174, *182*
Ghiselin, N., 57, 61, *182*
Gilbert, R., 159, *182*
Gordon, R., 62, 123, *182*
Gordon, W. J. J., 98, 104, 145, *182*
Gowan, J. C., 4, 47, 48, 50, 55, 151, *182*
Graves, M., 173, *182*
Green, H. A., 173, 174, *182*
Grippen, V. B., 4, *182*
Guilford, J. P., 4, 5, 10, 12, 13, 18, 20, 33, 34, 35, 42, 57, 92, 93, 94, 95, 136, 141, 172, 173, *182*

**H**

Hammdon-Turner, C., 50, *182*
Hemingway, E., 107, 150, *182*
Horn, C. C., 35, 173, *182*

**J**

Jaynes, J., 110, *182*
Johnson, D. L., 31, *182*
Jorgensen, A. N., 173, 174, *182*
Jung, C. G., 47, *182*

**K**

Kandinsky, W., 128, *182*
Kenneally, C., 112, *183*

Khatena, J., 3, 4, 5, 7, 10, 11, 12, 14, 15, 16, 17, 20, 21, 22, 27, 28, 29, 31, 37, 39, 42, 43, 44, 50, 70, 71, 72, 104, 115, 127, 136, 138, 151, 152, 154, 171, 177, 178, *182, 183, 184*
Khatena, N., 62, 70, 71, 72, *183*
Knauber, A., 35, *183*
Kogan, N., 10, *184*
Kohl, D., 62, 174, *181*
Krippner, S., 55, *184*
Krishna, G., 56, *183*

**L**
Land, G., 43, 58, 83, 112, 113, 142, *183*
Lehman, H. C., 4, *183*
Lowenfield, V., 34, 135, *184*

**M**
McCarter, W., 159, *182*
McKellar, P., 57, *183*
Meeker, M. N., 136, *183*
Meier, N. C., 35, 173, *183*
Morse, D. T., 5, 27, 31, 37, 171, 178, *183*

**N**
Noller, R. B., 100, *183*

**O**
Ornstein, R., 110, *183*
Osborn, A. F., 98, 99, 128, *183*

**P**
Parnes, S. J., 4, 94, 98, 99, 100, 172, *183*
Preble, D., 54, 62, 84, 128, *183*
Preble, S., 84, 128, *183*
Prince, G. M., 107, *184*

**R**
Rhodes, M., 5, 9, 10, 27, 28, *184*

Rimm, S., 59, *183*
Rockenstein, Z., 56, *184*
Rossman, J., 4, 95, 96, *184*
Rubin, W., 116, 128, *184*
Rugg, H., 58, *184*

**S**
Sargent, W., 159, 163, *184*
Schaefer, C. E., 29, *184*
Simonton, D. K., 45, *184*
Starkweather, E. K., 42, *184*
Stoney, B., 109, *184*
Sugg, R., Jr., 116, *184*
Sullivan, H. S., 47, *184*

**T**
Taylor, C. W., 28, 29, 31, *184*
Tillyard, E. M., 82, *184*
Torrance, E. P., 4, 5, 6, 7, 10, 12, 13, 19, 22, 27, 28, 29, 35, 37, 42, 154, *183, 184*

**V**
Vargiu, J., 95, 96, 97, 111, *184*

**W**
Wallach, M. A., 10, *184*
Wallas, G., 4, 56, 58, 95, 96, 100, 101, 111, *184*
White, J., 55, *184*
Wilson, B., 36, *185*
Wilson, E., 123, *185*
Wilson, M., 36, *185*
Wordsworth, W., 3, 54, 61, 117, *185*

**Y**
Yates, W. B., 107, *185*

**Z**
Zelanski, P., 167, *185*
Zimmerman, E., 37, *181*

# Subject Index

## A

abstract art, 128
Advance Placement Program in Studio Art,
    36–37, 38
*An Artist's Color Wheel*, 165
analogical comparison, 3
analogical thinking, 43, 58, 78, 127
analogy-metaphor, 7, 47, 48, 50, 57, 58, 103,
    104–109, 112, 118, 125, 127, 145,
    146–151, 153, 154, 155, 157, 160, 176,
    176
appraisal or evaluation of artworks, 5, 170,
    171–179
Appraisal Rating Scale of Artwork, 177
approaches to appraise artworks, 175–176
art and imagery, 61, 62
art nouveau paintings, 128
art talent, 27, 32, 33–39, 115
Art Talent Assessment Record, 37–39
art texture, 166–169, 176
A-Thinking, 57

## B

Biographical Inventory Form U, 31

## C

cognition, 93, 94
color, 787, 86–87, 89, 101, 108, 123, 128, 131,
    132, 135, 144, 149, 151, 152, 153, 155,
    157, 159–170, 174
color afterimage, 166
color and light, 160, 176
color and value, 160–162, 176
color harmony, 159, 164–165
color properties, 16, 17, 64

color psychology 159, 166–167
color separation by prism, 162–163
color wheel, 159, 163–164, 165
communication, 48
conscious-preconscious-unconscious, 47–49, 56,
    104, 110, 122, 143, 144, 151-153, 167
cosmic, 49–51, 54
creating art, 41–42
creative and mental growth in children, 34
creative artistic imagination, 4
creative development, 1, 4
creative imagery, 3, 6, 174
creative imagination, 2, 3, 6, 22, 24, 32, 47, 50,
    51, 53–58, 59, 60, 61, 62, 78, 84, 90, 91,
    92, 95, 99, 103, 112, 115, 117, 122, 125,
    127, 128, 131, 145, 146, 154, 157, 167,
    174, 176
creative potential, 1, 5
creative problem solving, 4, 6, 7, 57, 59, 60, 61,
    95–100, 110–112, 172
creative problem solving in art, 100–101,
    110–112, 122, 125
creativity 1, 2, 4, 5, 7, 30, 33, 51, 115, 145, 172
creativity as group related, 4
creativity as individual, 4
creativity as nonverbal, 9
creativity as person, process, product, press, 5, 9,
    27
creativity as verbal, 9
creativity definitions 9, 10–13
creativity in jazz, 1, 2
creativity in poetry, 2–4
creativity in the visual arts, 33
creativity in various settings, 4
Creativity Tests for Children, 5, 13–19, 35, 37

creativogenic society, 45
criteria for judging art, 173–174
cubism, 128

**D**
design principles in art, 78, 81, 83–90, 95, 118–121, 124, 174, 176
divergent or creative thinking, 5, 7, 10, 12, 13–19, 33, 34, 35, 57, 91, 92–93, 95, 125, 127, 136–142, 176

**E**
educational implications of creativity, 5
"Egg Series," 76, 105
elaboration, 11, 12, 21, 33, 34, 35, 92–94
Elizabethan World Order, 81, 82
environment, 44, 45–46, 115–120, 123, 124, 127, 136, 144
environmental conditions, 4
evaluating products, 5
evaluation and judgment of art, 172–173, 174, 175, 176

**F**
figural and generic motifs, 59, 62–79, 81, 83, 109, 117, 118, 120–121, 123, 124, 125, 127, 128, 131, 132, 135, 136, 138, 139, 142, 143, 144, 145–146, 149, 151, 155, 157, 168, 176
flexibility, 10, 12, 21, 22, 33, 35, 92–93
fluency, 10, 92–93

**G**
general systems, 81, 82–83
gifted, 1, 4
Gifted and Talented Screening Form, 31
*Grow or Die*, 83, 143

**H**
hologram, 50, 55
Horn Art Aptitude Inventory, 35, 36, 173

**I**
Ideal Pupil Checklist, 28
ideal spiral, 70
identification of creativity, 1, 4, 5, 27
identification of talent, 27, 31
illusion, 166, 168, 176
imagery, 3, 33, 51, 53, 54, 59–62, 103, 108–112, 115, 145, 146, 152, 154, 156, 157, 164, 176
images, 2, 3, 43, 59–62, 115–116, 117, 122, 123, 127, 152–153, 155, 156, 157, 168

imaginative music, 2
individual, 46–49, 54, 120, 122, 127
intellectual abilities, 28, 91–94
intellectual and personality traits, 28
intuitive imagination, 56

**K**
Khatena–Morse Multitalent Perception Inventory, 5, 27, 31–32, 37, 38
Khatena–Torrance Creative Perception Inventory, 5, 29–31, 37, 38
Knauber Art Ability Test, 35, 36

**L**
language of discovery, 59–61
language of visual art, 33, 43, 48, 62, 109, 115, 116, 117, 118–121, 124, 145, 146, 156, 174, 176
lateral thinking, 6

**M**
measures of creativity, 5, 9–26
metaphorical thinking, 43, 58, 112, 125
motivation, 4, 6
Multidimensional Interactive Creative Imagination Model, 43–50, 59, 115–116, 127

**N**
natural rhythm, 2
nature of creativity, 1, 4, 5
nurture or training of creativity, 1, 4, 5, 6, 7

**O**
Onomatopoeia and Images, 22, 23–24, 154, 156
originality, 11, 12, 21, 22, 35, 42, 92–93, 146, 157
Oswald color system, 163

**P**
Pointillism technique, 166
primary imagination, 49, 55
prism experiments, 162–163
psi phenomenon, 56
psychic energy, 56
psychometric creativity, 4

**S**
secondary imagination, 55
Shapes Test, 42
social implications of creativity, 5
sociocultural creativity, 4, 116, 124
sociodrama, 7

Something About Myself, 29, 30, 31, 156
Sounds and Images, 22, 23, 24, 154
Structure of Intellect model, 5, 10, 13, 33, 34, 57, 92–94, 95, 125, 127 136, 137, 172
stylized art, 128–130, 160
synasthesia, 123
Synectics, 103–104
synthesis-destructuring-restructuring 7, 43, 47, 58, 78, 103, 112–114, 125, 127, 128, 143–144, 176

**T**
Talent in the Arts, 171, 178
talented, 1
Test Climate, 12–13
texture, 168
Thinking Creatively with Sounds and Words, 22–24, 42, 154, 156
thinking imagination, 57–58
Torrance Tests of Creative Thinking, 5, 19–22, 35, 37

touchstone, 42, 172
training approaches or programs, 4, 5, 6
transformation, 2, 10, 42, 51, 57, 58, 60, 78, 112, 113, 114, 117, 118, 123, 124, 127, 128, 142, 146, 148

**U**
unifying principles of transformation, 83, 112
unoriginal or common response, 25–26

**V**
visionizing, 100
visual narrative, 36, 144, 147, 148

**W**
Webster color system or wheel, 163, 164, 165
What Kind of Person Are You?, 29–30

**Z**
*Zeitgeist*, 45

# About the Authors

**Joe Khatena** is Professor and Head Emeritus of the Department of Educational Psychology and Professor Emeritus of Psychology at Mississippi State University. His appointments in the Department of Educational Psychology began in 1978 and continued until his retirement in 1991.

He earned his bachelor's degree at the University of Malaya, majoring in English. He holds a master's degree from the University of Singapore and a Ph.D. in psychology from the University of Georgia.

Joe Khatena served as a teacher in the public school system from 1950 to 1956; a lecturer in English and education from 1957 to 1965; Assistant Professor of Psychology at East Carolina University; and an associate professor (1969–1972) and full professor (1972–1977) in Educational Foundations at Marshall University. At various times, he also served as a visiting professor at several universities both in the United States and abroad. On his retirement, he served as a visiting professor in the Faculty of Education at the University of Malaya (1992–1993).

His interest in giftedness and creativity led to the development of *Thinking Creatively With Sounds and Words* (1973/1998), the *Khatena–Torrance Creative Perception Inventory* (1976/1998), and the *Khatena–Morse Multitalent Perception Inventory* (1994). Best known of his books are *The Creatively Gifted Child: Suggestions for Parents and Teachers* (1978), *Educational Psychology of the Gifted* (1982), *Imagery and Creative Imagination* (1984), *Gifted: Challenge and Response for Education* (1992), and *Enhancing Creativity of Gifted Children: A Guide for Parents and Teachers* (1999).

Joe Khatena was a member of many professional organizations, is a Fellow of the American Psychological Association, and a past president of the National Association for Gifted Children. He is listed in 23 biographical works, including *Who's Who in Frontier Science and Technology*, *Who's Who in America*, and the *Encyclopedia of Special Education*. Khatena is the recipient of several awards, including the NAGC

Distinguished Scholar Award and Distinguished Service Award, Distinguished Summer Lecturer of Texas Women's University, Marshall University Research Award, Phi Kappa Phi Research Award and, two Fulbright Senior Lectureships to India.

 **Nelly Khatena** was born in Sumatra and educated in the Convent of the Holy Infant Jesus both in Malaya and Singapore. Married to Joe Khatena, they have four children and three grandchildren. Her family has resided in the United States for more than 30 years.

Among her many interests is stage makeup, and for many years she served theatrical groups in Singapore as a makeup artist, with a repertoire of plays and operas that included Shakespeare, Dryden, Pirandello, and Spenser. She also plays the piano, and was a professional secretary for many years in several large British and American houses of commerce.

Her early interest in art found expression in original needlecraft, drawings, and paintings, with special emphasis on flowers, plants, birds, and related natural scenes. She received her education in art at Mississippi State University.

Among the honors and awards she has received are membership in Phi Kappa Phi (1985) and Outstanding Undergraduate Woman of the Year (1988) for excellence in academic achievement generally and original artwork specifically.

She is a charter member of the National Museum of Women in the Arts, and a member of the Mississippi Museum of Art.

In the past few years, Nelly Khatena has produced 141 art pieces, known as the "Egg Series," using the medium of colored pencils. Several of her works have been exhibited in the Mississippi Museum of Art in Jackson (1985), and nearly all of them in one-person shows at the Meridian Museum of Art (1986) and the Pegasus Art Gallery of Mississippi State University (1987). At the time of the exhibitions, Kay Culper of *The Meridian Star* reported on her exhibited artworks in a feature entitled "Women and Visions" in 1986, and Norma Williamson did a feature of her in a lifestyles column in 1987. Khatena's international artworks were also exhibited at the Guaranty Deposit Bank in Starkville, Mississippi.

An original artwork entitled *Genesis* appeared on the book cover of *Imagery and Creative Imagination*, written by Joe Khatena and published in 1984 by Bearly Limited, in association with the Creative Education Foundation in Buffalo, New York. Another work, entitled *Strawberry Patch*, served as the cover design on a 1986 issue of the *Journal of Creative Behavior*. In addition, her work entitled *Sunburst* was selected by the International Student Association of Mississippi State University for imprinting on T-shirts for its International Fiesta of 1992.

Nelly Khatena is also coauthor of a significant paper in 1990 entitled "Metaphor Motifs and Creative Imagination in Art," published in the journal *Metaphor and Symbolic Activity* and author of a paper entitled "Art and Creative Imagination," published in *Gifted Education International*.

Professor Brent Funderburk, a well-known artist and head of the art department at Missisippi State University, comments about her work:

> Nelly's work approaches the intensity of expression in idea progression that is akin to that of visionaries such as William Blake, Buffalo's own Charles Burchfield, as well as Vincent Van Gogh. She empowers her images with a great understanding of visual analogies. These are states through each dimension of perception; the grace of line; color; value and texture; and pattern. The overall effect invites meditation and quest.

The Creative Education Foundation has invited Nelly Khatena for the past several years to serve as leader in its Summerfest Annual Creative Problem Solving Institute (CPSI) held at State University of New York in Buffalo. There, she makes many presentations of her philosophy of art through her work in slide shows. She is held in high regard by the leaders of CPSI and the membership of the Creative Education Foundation.

Her superior talent and originality led Dr. E. Paul Torrance, Alumni Foundation Distinguished Professor of the University of Georgia and internationally known for his contributions on creativity, to describe her "Egg Series" as "something unique and beautiful." In October 1990, she was also invited to present her artwork at the University of Georgia in the E. Paul Torrance annual lecture series.

She has presented her works and given lectures at universities and to the general public in Australia, India, South Africa, the People's Republic of China, Japan, Singapore, and Malaysia, where she was acclaimed as a highly creative artist with a fresh, unique, and stimulating perspective.

Drawing from her sensitive observations of nature and its rhythms and patterns, Nelly Khatena transforms the ordinary into the beautiful. Her use of metaphor, analogy and illusion in art is superbly illustrated in the imaginatively provocative "Egg Series." Cited in *Imagery and Creative Imagination* (Khatena, 1984) as showing "insightful application of the process of analogy and transformation," (p. 200), Nelly Khatena makes the magic and mystery of creative imagination accessible through her "Egg Series" in yet another way.